The Farmer's Wife Pony Club

SAMPLER QUILT

THE FARMER'S WIFE PONY CLUB QUILT 96″ × 105″
Designed and hand pieced by the author. Machine quilted by Nell Coons, Verona, WI.

The Farmer's Wife Pony Club

Sampler Quilt

Letters from the
Lucky Pony Winners of 1915
and 90 blocks that tell their stories

Laurie Aaron Hird

Dunbarton Press, LLC
Shullsburg, WI
thefarmerswifequilt.blogspot.com

15 14 13 12 11   6 5 4 3 2

Editor/Project Manager/Lead Designer: Toni Toomey
Technical Editor/Copy Editor: Barbara F. Smith
Proofreader: Amy R. Burdick
Cover and Interior Design/Technical Illustration: Toni Toomey
Photo Enhancement: Barbara F. Smith
Cover Art Digitizing: Jason Ullery

Quilt Photography: Dale Hall Photography dalehallphotography.com
Production: Fine Print Art & Editorial Services, staff@fineprintservices.com
Print Services: Oceanic Graphic Printing (USA), Inc., nj@ogprinting.com
Thanks to: Minnesota Historical Society Museum

The quilt design in this book may be used to create items for sale or display. At the author's request, on each item for sale, please attach a label with the following information: "Quilt design copyright © 2011 by Laurie Aaron Hird, from the book *The Farmer's Wife Pony Club Sampler Quilt.*"

Publisher's Cataloging in Publication Data

Hird, Laurie Aaron, 1956 –
The farmer's wife pony club sampler quilt: letters from the lucky pony winners of 1915 and 90 blocks that tell their stories/Laurie Aaron Hird. – 1st ed.

    p. cm.

Includes index.
ISBN 978-0-9829104-7-4

1. Patchwork. 2. Quilting. 3. Shetland Pony – Juvenile Literature. 4. Shetland Pony.
5. Children – United States – History – 20th Century – Bibliography. I. Lucky Pony Winners. II. Title.

746.46 – dc22

2011923987

DUNBARTON PRESS, LLC
SHULLSBURG, WI
thefarmerswifequilt.blogspot.com

Dedication

To my very dear family who has helped me with their love,
understanding, encouragement, and support:

My husband Steven, and our children and their spouses

Amy and her husband Adam

Elizabeth and her late husband Jared

Ruthanne and her husband Matthew

Timothy and his wife Katherine

and Leah, Josiah, Stephen, Laura, Seth, Martha, and Mary

In Memory of My Beloved Son-in-Law
Jared Scott Eggemeyer
(March 11, 1982-July 16, 2009)
Precious in the sight of the Lord is the death of His saints. Psalms 116:15
We rejoice, knowing that we will see our "Little Texas Buddy" again.

Acknowledgments

My sincere thanks to:

Toni Toomey of Fine Print Art & Editorial Services for sharing my vision for this book and bringing it to life with her design, layout, and illustrations. For putting together a team of talented professionals, who worked tirelessly to make this book as perfect and beautiful as humanly possible. In no way could I have done this without her, nor would I have wanted to.

Barbara Smith of BF Smith Images for her work enhancing scans of the nearly century-old Pony Club Winner photographs. For her eagle-eyed technical edit and meticulous copy edit—a very big job on a project of this length and complexity.

Nell Coons, of Verona, Wisconsin, for another one of her unique and beautiful quilting designs.

Dale Hall of Dale Hall Photography for photographing THE FARMER'S WIFE PONY CLUB QUILT so clearly that I feel like I can reach out and touch each block.

The members of the FarmersWifeSampler Yahoo! Group for their advice and encouragement and, most of all, their friendship.

Additional thanks go to:

Vicki Lynne Fischer of Nancy Zieman Productions, who was the first to listen to my Pony Club idea and encourage me, and to Nancy Zieman for her support, warmth, and thoughtfulness.

Penny McMorris at The Electric Quilt Company for patiently answering my many technical questions.

Dean Sherman, Kim Liou, and Barbara Zee at Oceanic Graphic Printing. They gave this project the same superb service and attention they give their "big" clients.

Eric Mortenson, Photo Lab Supervisor at the Minnesota Historical Society Museum of St. Paul, Minnesota, for his help in obtaining the Pony Club Winners photographs.

About The Farmer's Wife Pony Club

In 1907 Edward A. Webb, the publisher of *The Farmer's Wife* magazine, decided to appoint his India-born, missionary-trained sister to the position of editor. One of Ella S. Webb's first decisions was to begin a contest that would prove to be the magazine's most famous and successful. Miss Webb's plan was to hire young children to sell subscriptions to their magazine. The subscription prices were quite reasonable for the time: three years for $.50, five years for $.75, and seven years for $1.00.

In exchange for the children's efforts, they received prizes, such as bicycles, talking machines, cameras, and rifles. It can only be supposed, however, that most of the children were working for the grand prize, a Shetland pony, along with a saddle, bridle, and often, a carriage. In 1907, the company had created The Farmer's Wife Pony Club for children who wanted to compete for prizes.

In the early years of their pony-club contest, the company had a credibility problem. While trying to obtain subscriptions, the children were often told that the contest was not genuine—that they would never receive the much hoped-for Shetland pony. To prove the contest's authenticity, the editors asked the children to send in photographs of themselves with their ponies. Over one hundred children sent thank you letters with their photographs.

The Farmer's Wife Pony Club ended twelve years later in 1918, but not before they had given away over 500 ponies to grateful boys and girls all across America.

Webb Publishing Co. announced their first pony contest in the March 1907 issue.

CONTENTS

INTRODUCTION

How I Came to
Write This Book

My *story begins* in the mid 1990s when my family and I were living in a small Wisconsin town. I wanted to live in the country and would often check out books about homesteading at my local library. It was during this time that I found a small booklet published in 1922 by *The Farmer's Wife* magazine. The title, "Do You Want Your Daughter to Marry a Farmer?" intrigued me and made me smile. The booklet was a collection of letters written by farm wives in answer to that question. I loved the letters and knew they were special. I copied them and stored them in my file cabinet.

More than a decade later, on my birthday, I found myself at the doctor's office with a present I did not want. I had a recurring foot injury that would not heal, so the doctor gave me a large, heavy, black-metal boot to wear. I was upset and disappointed that I would have to cancel the summertime activities with my family and spend the time sitting in a chair with my boot on! During the school year, I home school my children, which, as you can imagine, keeps me busy. So the prospect of sitting idle all summer was not pleasant.

I prayed that the Lord would give me something to do while I unhappily sat in a chair. While visiting

May 1915 issue of *The Farmer's Wife* magazine, published from 1903 to 1939.

a fabric store two weeks later, I discovered Rosemary Youngs' book, *The Civil War Diary Quilt*. On the long drive home, it occurred to me that I could pair farm-themed quilt blocks with the collection of farm wives' letters that I had filed away years before.

Within the next few days, the details of my book idea fell into place, and I began to work in earnest on my secret. You see, I didn't want to tell my friends and family, because who would believe that I wanted to write a quilt book! I kept my secret for nearly a year and finally told everyone after I was offered a contract to write *The Farmer's Wife Sampler Quilt*.

While I was working on the book, I began to collect *The Farmer's Wife* magazines, which were published between 1903 and 1939. The magazines contain a fascinating and unique look at life in that period from a country-woman's perspective. In the earlier issues, I often came across articles and pictures of something called "The Farmer's Wife Pony Club," "The Shetland Pony Club," or simply, "The Pony Club."

It was a year later, when I acquired a rare copy of a small "Lucky Pony Winners" booklet that I finally understood what this pony club was all about.

Children had been invited by the Webb Publishing Company to join the Pony Club and compete to win the Grand Prize of a pony, saddle, and car-riage by selling subscriptions to the magazine. The pony winners were asked to send photos of their ponies, but some children also sent letters. The letters and photographs were published in *The Farmer's Wife* magazine and in small "Lucky Pony Winners" booklets like the one I had acquired. With this booklet in hand, the idea for my second book was born. But this time, it wasn't a secret.

Second "Lucky Pony Winners" booklet, published in 1913, with 30 letters and photos of 36 children and ponies.

Planning Your Quilt

A Lot of Play and a Little Work

This is a playful quilt. I had fun with it from start to finish—selecting the blocks and the fabrics, and sewing the quilt.

I had the quilt photographed in two stages for this book, which added some extra steps in sewing it. Instead of assembling the whole quilt at one time, first I sewed it together in sections of either six or nine blocks. Then I took these sections to the photographer, who did close-up "flat shots" of the sections. These were used throughout the book for the individual block photos.

I must admit this step wasn't much fun. But that's only because time was running out, and I had to hurry. Back home after the first photo shoot, I went to work rearranging some of the sections and then finished assembling the quilt top.

Next, I sent it off to be machine quilted then took it back to the photographer for the final whole-quilt shot. Since you can skip these extra steps, I hope that you will have at least as much fun making this quilt as I did, and maybe even more.

I sewed the blocks into sections for the first round of photography.

My Block–Selection Rules

Before I could decide on the block designs, I had to choose the Lucky Pony Winner letters that would go in the book. First, I went through the letters and eliminated the ones that were too short—just a few lines. Next, I wanted to pick blocks with just the right names to go with the letters.

Sometimes, I was able to find a block with the same name as the pony, such as *Sunshine* (letter on page 64) or *Pansy* (letter on page 138). Other times, the block name included the child's name, such as *Crystal Star* (letter on page 60) or *John's Favorite* (letter on page 130). A few times, the place where the child lived was used, as in *North Carolina Beauty* (letter on page 122) and *New York* (letter on page 134). But most often it was something the child said in the letter that caused me to pick a particular block. Two of my favorites are *Confederate Rose* (letter on page 52) and *Patience Corners* (letter on page 140).

Now here's a mystery for you to solve: It took my eagle-eyed copy editor to notice that one block in the quilt does not follow any of my reasons for choosing the names. Can you find which block doesn't fit my rules?

Sunshine

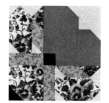
Pansy

Crystal Star

John's Favorite

North Carolina Beauty

New York

Confederate Rose

Patience Corners

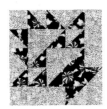

Cake Stand

Pig's Tail

My Fabric–Selection Rules

I reviewed the letters again before choosing my fabrics. I used many western, pony, and country prints, and some others that might surprise you. For instance, there is a candy print in *Cake Stand* (letter on page 56) and an apple print in *Pig's Tail* (letter on page 106). My seemingly strange choices will make sense when you read the accompanying letters.

Although I used novelty prints for THE FARMER'S WIFE PONY CLUB QUILT, it can be sewn using any type of print—from reproduction prints, to batiks, to orientals. Some of the novelty prints I used in this quilt are out of date, so it's quite likely they will no longer be available. However, new novelty prints with horse themes are usually available as the older ones are discontinued.

Perhaps you want your quilt to look just like mine. That would be difficult, since the fabrics in a scrap quilt would be close to impossible to duplicate. However, if you want to go for the same overall visual effect, you can use the "rules" I set for myself when I began sewing THE FARMER'S WIFE PONY CLUB QUILT.

A note on supporting our local shops: When looking for fabric, as much as possible, I prefer to support my local quilt and fabric shops. But if I need to go online, I usually begin my search on eBay. I have found the vendors to be a great resource for purchasing fat quarters, since I rarely need larger cuts of fabric.

I only had a few rules. First, I wanted to use cheerful and colorful novelty prints in mostly primary colors. The only color that I decided not to use was pink. Second, it was important for me to include yellow and orange, or the quilt would have been too dark and dull.

I did not plan my fabric choices for the entire quilt ahead of time, but rather block by block. After I had sewn several blocks, I would lay them out and evaluate them to see if I had used one color too much, or another not enough. I would make this evaluation several times throughout and would plan my next color choices accordingly.

No matter what color scheme you prefer, don't forget to use a zinger fabric here and there. It adds sparkle to the blocks and the overall quilt. I used various yellows throughout the quilt. But bright yellows, like the ones In *Jewel* and *Railroad Crossing* became my zingers of choice for this quilt.

While choosing my fabrics, I also kept two classic guidelines in mind: contrast in value (difference between lights and darks) and contrast in scale (difference between large and small prints). For the most part, it is best for each block to range from a medium contrast, such as *Girl's Joy* and *Morning Star*, to a strong contrast, such as *Village School House* and *Cat's Paw*. Though I aim for strong contrast when I select the fabrics, some blocks, such as *Betty's Delight*, turn out without much difference between the lights and darks. I call these

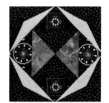

Jewel   *Railroad Crossing*

Girl's Joy   *Morning Star*

Village School House   *Cat's Paw*

Betty's Delight

blocks "mushy" and have found that leaving a few of these low-contrast blocks help to tone a sampler quilt down a bit. I have also found that it is not necessary to plan these "mushy" blocks, they just happen.

Choosing fabrics for contrast of scale was easy to do for this quilt. If the pieces of the block were large, I was able to use larger-scale prints. While small pieces looked best with small-scale prints. *Rambling Road* and *Star of Hope* are examples of creating contrast by mixing large- and small-scale fabrics. *Children's Delight* and *Country Lanes* have both contrast of value and contrast of scale.

I hope you will make up your own fabric-selection rules, remembering to include contrast of scale and contrast of value, and then have fun making your own unique fabric choices.

Practice Need Not Make "Perfect"

Making a sampler quilt is a learning experience. I was not an accomplished quilter when I began my first book, *The Farmer's Wife Sampler Quilt*, but since finishing THE FARMER'S WIFE PONY CLUB QUILT, I believe that there are not many blocks that would perplex me. However, no matter how much I practice, my blocks do not always come out "perfect." Take *Cowboy's Star*, for example. That was my second attempt with that particular block.

My first attempt was sitting happily in my trash can. (At least, *I* was happy it was there!) Imagine my dismay when my second attempt was finished and I noticed that only three of my star points were black! I could have changed it, but decided

to leave it, since perfection is not necessary in quilting.

Enjoy making this quilt and learn as you go. Your quilt does not have to be perfect; just make it your own.

Rambling Road

Star of Hope

Children's Delight

Country Lanes

Cowboy's Star

About Your Shetland Pony

Over in Shetland Islands, just north of Scotland, where these ponies come from, they live on terms of the most intimate friendship with their owners and their families. Not infrequently when one is in a particularly social mood, he strolls through the door of the little cottage and is treated like a member of the household. Not knowing the meaning of unkind treatment, he comes to believe in man as his natural friend and benefactor.

The stock of ponies in the islands is never large, for the demand by American breeders and those of other countries is greater every season than the supply of animals available for export purposes. Some six hundred ponies are produced annually on the islands, and they sell for about fifty dollars each, which, added to the cost of transportation and the duty, which in this country is thirty dollars, makes the imported stock fairly expensive.

Ponies may be purchased immediately after they are weaned, when five or six months old. Their home can be as simple as a lightly constructed shed if free from dampness. The expense of feeding them is so small that it hardly need be considered. During the summer, one animal will be able to get practically all his living on the lawn around the house. By the time the pony is fifteen months of age, he may be driven to a moderate extent and becomes an indispensable member of the family, often living to be thirty or forty years of age.

— from the 1915 *Lucky Pony Winners booklet*

No Child is Too Small to Make Friends With a Shetland Pony

Using This
Book and CD

The blocks in this book range from easy to challenging. For some blocks, beginning quilters may want help from more experienced quilters.

The section, **Assembly Diagrams and Cutting Lists**, beginning on page 184, gives you all the information you need for making each block.

Block Assembly Diagrams

The key to "reading" an assembly diagram is understanding the width of the spaces between the pieces.

First, if there are no spaces shown between the pieces, it means they can be sewn together in any order. These units should be sewn first. Second, join the units and pieces with the narrowest spaces between them.

Continue joining pieces and units in order from the narrowest spaces to the widest. *Country Lanes* is one of the easiest diagrams to follow, but if you stick to the assembly order from narrowest to widest, you'll be able to figure out any of the diagrams.

There are a number of blocks, such as *Cowboy's Star*, that have inset seams. Trust me, the diagram is correct.

Cowboy's Star
assembly diagram

Country Lanes
assembly diagram

Cutting Instructions

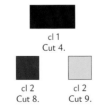

cl 1
Cut 4.

cl 2
Cut 8.

cl 2
Cut 9.

Cutting instructions

Each assembly diagram has thumbnail drawings of the pieces, labeled with the number of the template (found on the CD) and the number of pieces to cut.

CD Contents

Each block assembly diagram page has a set of icons showing what's available on the CD for that block. The next section, ***What's on the CD,*** explains the contents of the CD and gives some tips on how to use it.

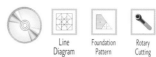

Icons show CD contents for each block.

What's on the CD?

*T*he CD for this book comes packed with new content, thanks to the generous feedback from the readers of my first book. As I have come to learn, there is more than one way to cut and piece a block. I prefer using templates, while many prefer rotary cutting, and others prefer foundation piecing. Insofar as the pieces in the blocks permit, I have incorporated all of these different preferences into the contents of the CD.

Templates

All of the blocks can be cut from templates. The templates for each block are placed together and can be printed out on one or two sheets of paper.

You may have noticed that wherever the name of a block appears in the book, it is accompanied by a pair of initials set in parentheses. The initials are unique to that block. The labels on the templates for a block include its initials. As I cut the fabric pieces, I pin the labeled templates to the pieces so, I can identify which block they belong to.

Rotary–Cutting Measurements

For those who prefer rotary cutting, I have provided measurements for pieces that can be cut to the nearest one-eighth inch. If a block has only one piece that can be rotary cut, that measurement has been given. These measurements are provided for all of the blocks in one table at the beginning of the CD.

Foundation Patterns

Foundation piecing is preferred by many quilters, because it allows for greater accuracy with points. Some blocks in this book cannot be foundation pieced at all. However, most can be pieced in sections, which can then be sewn together. The CD contains foundation sections for any blocks that can be pieced in sections.

Line Diagrams

Many quilters like line diagrams like the ones in books that provide no other options for cutting pieces for a block. I think between the templates, rotary-cutting measurements, and foundation patterns, most readers' needs will be met. However, my illustrator assured me that line diagrams wouldn't take long to produce, so they are included on the CD.

Printing Templates, Patterns, and Diagrams

The contents of the CD were drawn to print to the correct size and fit on 81/2" × 11" paper. To make the templates print at full size, depending on your printer, set page scaling at "None" or "100%." If there is a setting for Paper Position, set it at "Centered." If you can't find a paper position setting, it may mean the paper is centered by default and no other options are available. For help, refer to the Owner's Manual that came with your printer.

THE FARMER'S WIFE PONY CLUB QUILT 96″ × 105″
Designed and hand pieced by the author. Machine quilted by Nell Coons, Verona, WI.

1

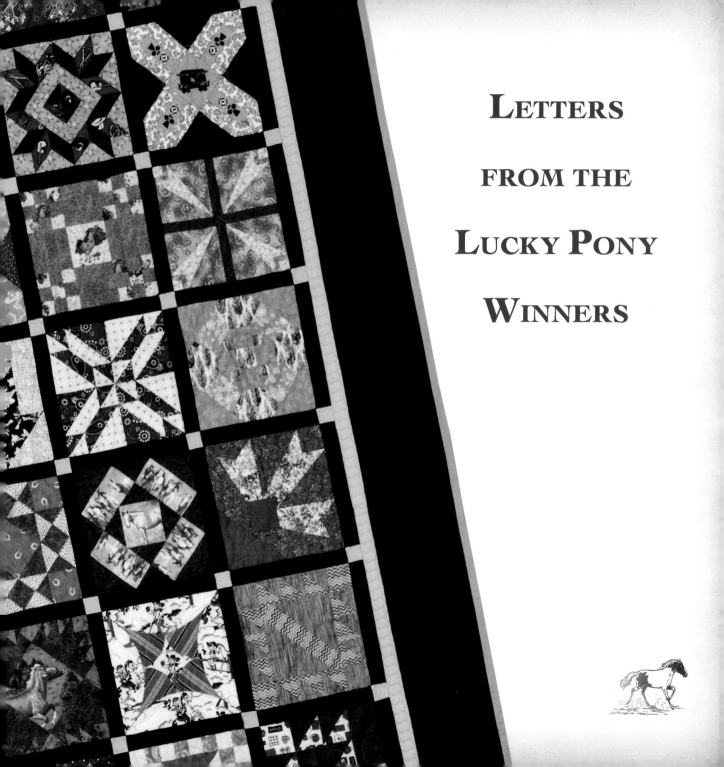

LETTERS FROM THE LUCKY PONY WINNERS

*O*ne evening I was looking through The Farmer's Wife and I saw a picture of a pony all hitched up ready for a drive. I had always wanted a pony so I read it over and over. It told how a boy or girl could win a pony without paying a cent. Oh! how delighted I was to know any little boy could have a pony. I asked papa what he thought of it. He just smiled and said: "Try if you like." So I entered the contest and began to work.

Some of my friends tried to discourage me; they said there is no use trying, it was only a fake; others said to do my best for the contest was perfectly fair and all right.

Soon came the close of the contest and I mailed my last subscriptions that night. Finally Sunday morning came and the postmaster received the news that I had won. But, Oh dear, the Webb Publishing Company thought me a girl as the notice to the postmaster stated a little girl by the name of Amyle Kafer had won a pony by the name of "Bonnie." And how disappointed I was; I laughed and I cried to think I was not the one to win one of those beautiful ponies. After I had read the notice over several times I began to think it was only a mistake and that they had taken me for a girl. It was the best news that ever came to me. I cannot tell how glad I was that I would receive a dandy Shetland Pony.

How delighted I was to know I would have my pony Christmas day for Grandma always

A Dandy (ad)

has a turkey Christmas and all the grandchildren would be there and I could show off my pony in great style. But Christmas came and no pony and the next day, the next and next. I met every train, I could not give it up. Wednesday was a beautiful day, the sun seemed so bright and all the birds seemed so happy. I did not care to go to the depot. I was so down-hearted I began to think it was a fake. But my playmates said: "We won't give up, I know she will sure come today." We strolled down the back way so the men and boys up on the streets would not see us. It was just time when we reached the depot for the westbound train. The train pulled in and the car door was opened and in it was a pony crate with a little black Shetland pony. I rushed to the car and on the crate was my name. How my heart beat with joy! I can not tell how, but I was in the express car before the express man could unloosen her. She was so nice and tame and we uncrated her at once. I mounted her and rode up through Main Street calling to everyone I saw, "Here is my pony, I knew she would come."

continued on next page

"Bonnie" Taking Amyle and His Friends Hunting

continued

I used to live in town. On our place, we had an awful large barn. I tell you it wasn't much fun to help keep it clean until "Bonnie" came. But she made things different. I throw down enough hay for the other horses and I feed them too. I did not know what to do with myself at vacation. I used to be so lonesome but when "Bonnie" came there was plenty of boys around to help me ride her. Sometimes we play circus and then she is the race horse, we would ride around the house and barn and play that was our race track. Sometimes I would try to ride standing up on her back, but that didn't work very often because I would slip to the ground. It didn't hurt much though as I did not have far to fall. I just jumped. The boys all like me better since I got "Bonnie." They let me play with their toys now and I think I like the other boys better, too. I used to go after the milk in the evenings with my brother on ahead of me, or if I wanted to I could ride over to my grandfather's farm and get a big dinner and "Bonnie" would get a big dinner too.

I am only nine years old and I started to school when I was five years old. It is one and a half miles from my home to school and how tired I would get. But now I do not mind that as I have my Shetland Pony to ride. This little pony is about 43 inches high, so that although I am not very tall I can get on her back quite easily. At school I tie "Bonnie" to a tree so that she can eat grass.

Home Treasure (ht)

At recess the children like to play with "Bonnie." At noon I ride her home to dinner and then back to school. If the children have candy or cookies they have to be careful or the pony will get them. She will, sometimes, go by herself on Saturdays. She is not much like us boys, we like to stay out. I could not part with my pony for she is the treasure of my heart and I just love her with all my heart. Anyone could not help liking her she is so pretty and shiny black.

She will follow us boys wherever we go. She loves to be in the orchard and eat apples. I haul the cans of buttermilk from the house to the pigs and I haul the corn to the horses. I and "Bonnie"

Starting for the Parade

have plenty to do now and I like the farm better than town. There wouldn't have been any fun in anything if it hadn't been for "Bonnie." She did it all. She made me like town better when I lived there, now she makes me like the farm best.

Just as soon as I wake up in the morning I think of "Bonnie" and the good time I am going to have with her that day and then when I go to sleep at night I go to sleep thinking about what fun all us boys had with her going hunting or riding races or all the things we did.

If only lots of other boys and girls could have a pony like "Bonnie" I am sure they would be very happy for a pony is the best chum ever. And I also want to say that the Webb Publishing Company used me fine and did everything just as they said they would.

Dear Little "Snuggles"
Alberta and Florence Ashdown, Chemung Co., New York

How can we ever thank you enough for dear little "Snuggles?" He is the loveliest little pony. Little sister and I can do most anything with him. We ride him all over now.

One day I lay a pillow under his head while he was sleeping and the next time he lay down he put his head right on that pillow.

My pony eats everything but strawberries and onions. I think he might like onions only they smell so awful.

I am so sorry I cannot send some more pictures of "Beauty" but we could not get pictures taken.

We live quite a ways from town and could not find any one to come out, so had to give it up and now "Beauty" is away from home. Papa put her in pasture 27 miles away for a few weeks. She has a dear little baby pony, spotted black and white, three weeks old. It is so cute. I would like to have had both their pictures to send to you.

I want to tell you about the time I went camping with "Beauty."

One day papa decided that we would all camp out at Lake Senatchurne, for a couple of days; he said that if we went I could drive "Beauty."

The day before we started we packed all the things we needed and laid out our clothes. We got up at four o'clock in the morning, and I started a little ahead of the rest, because I thought the other two horses could go faster than "Beauty."

I started at seven o'clock in the morning and drove the twenty miles in four hours. We ate our dinner and got settled down by three o'clock.

Papa and I went in a boat and put out a trout line. We didn't catch any fish in time for our supper. The next morning mamma and I went down to Sandy Beach to fish. I caught the only two fish caught by hand, a catfish and a sunfish. When we got back, we went to our trout line. By the moving of the trout line papa knew that we had a big fish. When we got it in the boat, we found that it was a black bass. It was the largest black

A Beauty (ab)

bass ever caught in that lake. It weighed six and one-fourth pounds.

In the afternoon I started home. I started at four o'clock—it was eight o'clock when I got home. One mile and a half from our place I met an engine. I was coming down a hill when suddenly "Beauty" turned out of the road into the ditch. I looked to see why she turned out and saw the engine in the road. If she hadn't turned out I would have been run over, for I couldn't see the engine because it was so dark. Mamma and papa never caught up with me until I was turning into the lane leading to the house. It was the best time I ever had, and I have had hundreds of good times since the Webb Publishing Company sent me "Beauty."

Bert with Sisters Ferne, Eileen and Ona, and Baby Max Ready for a Ride

"BONNIE BETSY"
CLEIGHTON ELDRIDGE DAVIS, CAMPBELL CO., TENNESSEE

I must tell you some of the cute tricks she will do. She will walk right up the steps onto the porch and wants to go into the house, and upon finding the screen opened "Betsy" just walked in and made herself at home, or welcome to a pitcher of lemonade setting on the dining table that mamma had prepared for supper and she simply refused to go out until she had finished the lemonade and then some sugar was presented her in order to get her out doors.

I want to write and tell you how glad I was when I received word that I was one of the "Lucky Pony Winners" in the Contest that closed September 30th, 1912, and what good times I have had with my pony, "Tramp." He is brown and white and weighs 300 pounds. Everyone tells me that he is the cutest and smallest pony they ever saw. I have had several chances to sell him, but would not like to part with him at any price. He is larger and fatter than he was when he came and as slick as a mole.

I was at school when the letter came telling me I was a winner, and when I got home, mamma told me that papa wanted me at the barn. I ran out to the barn and papa told me he was fixing up a place to keep "Tramp" in. My, but I was the happiest boy you ever saw. I went to the train twice to meet him but he did not come, but the next day papa went and he was there. Everybody around town was at the depot to see him. He came the 15th of October and I have had lots of fun with him ever since.

I want to thank you ever so much for the beautiful outfit. It is surely a nice present and I don't see how you can give away such fine outfits for so little pay.

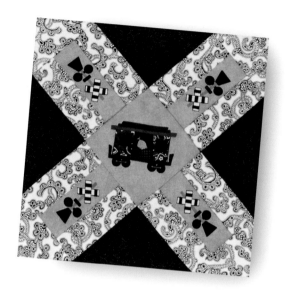

At the Depot (at)

Keith and "Tramp"

10

What I sent in was not a tenth part of what the outfit cost.

During the winter I could not drive him much, but since the roads got good we drive him to school every day. At night all the boys and girls want to ride with me. My cousin is visiting me now and we have lots of fun. When I have "Tramp" turned out in the orchard and he sees me coming after him he commences to shake his head and paw in the ground with his left foot. This morning I thought I would have a little horseback ride, but "Tramp" did not think so, so he tried to throw me off. He would rear up on his hind feet and then kick up. Once I nearly went over his head. When he throws us off, he always stops as soon as we are off and seems to laugh at us and waits for us to get on again. I drove him to a picnic the other day and had a good time. He feels fine now and I like to drive him. He likes apples, candy and all such things to eat. He bites me sometimes when I play with him, but not hard enough to hurt.

I can never thank the Webb Publishing Company enough for sending me such a nice playmate.

"We Drive 'Tramp' to School Every Day"

11

Last Fall when I started out to win my pony, "Cute," most of the people told me it was a fake scheme of the paper people to get subscriptions, but when, on Christmas day, my pony came by express, they sang a different tune and now they say, "Well, the Webb people are honest and did not fool you." Daddy went to town and brought "Cute" home and put him by our Christmas tree and then called sister and me to see him and I said, "Oh daddy, what a beautiful pony!" I was the happiest little girl in the world. "Cute" was welcomed by the whole family, and we all have learned to love him very much. He looked like a big Teddy Bear in his long winter coat but now he is nice and slick and fat as a ball of butter.

He eats apples, sugar and oranges, and when he wants a drink he whinnies to us and after he drinks all he wants, he will tip the bucket over with his nose. He opens the kitchen door and will come in and look around and when I tell him to go out, he will whinny at me as if to say, "I want something to eat." I have lots of pleasure driving him and would not part with him for a lot of money. The other day a man offered to trade an auto for my pony and outfit but I

Arizona (az)

"Cute" and Leota

would not trade as I can have more fun with "Cute" and my buggy.

Everyone who has seen my pony has told me that he is the smallest and dearest pony they ever saw. "Cute" is only 40 inches high and weighs 250 pounds, so you see he is "cute" and small and a dandy little animal. All of my little chums like him and want to ride him. Among his tricks are pulling my hair ribbon off and untying my shoe laces. He is not afraid of trains or autos but it makes him awfully mad to have a boy ride beside him on a bike.

I wish every boy and girl could have a pony like mine and then they would have some dandy times. We live in a mountainous country but it does not seem to hurt "Cute's" wind, as he pulled me to Lead last week and back home again. Lead is about four miles from here so he traveled eight miles, but he was not a bit tired. We are planning to move down to Arizona, some time this winter and when we get there I intend to say a good word for the Webb Publishing Company to everybody I meet as they are certainly good to boys and girls by giving them darling little Shetland ponies. Of course I am going to take "Cute" with me to Arizona as I would not part with him for anything.

All Ready for Our Afternoon Ride

I received "Pedro" on New Year's day and I want to write and tell you of the good times I have had with him.

When my folks heard "Pedro" had come to town, papa at once hitched up a team for the wagon and went in to meet him in spite of the bad snow storm we had on that day. I could not understand why papa drove in to town in such weather and they would not tell me either, so when I came down in the barn that night, oh! I jumped with joy. There stood my darling pony in the barn.

"Pedro" is the cutest little Shetland Pony I ever saw and all my friends say so too. I feel as if I were the happiest boy in the country just on account of "Pedro."

I have a little sister seven years old and I think she likes the pony just as much as I do. We often go horse back riding and oh how nice "Pedro" trots. He seems to go faster than any of our large horses. Once a man on horseback with a fast trotting horse came over here and wanted me to race with him, so I at once saddled up "Pedro" and was ready, and am only too glad to tell you that I easily won the race.

Last summer papa got me a bicycle, but have made very little use of it since "Pedro" came. I drive home the cows with "Pedro" and whenever mamma asks me to go on an errand, I just throw the saddle on "Pedro" and off I go and get back in a short time. How nice not to have to walk!

"Pedro" seems to understand everything I say.

Apple Tree (ap)

Whenever I call him he runs right up to me and he will lie down if I tell him and shake hands whenever I reach him my hand. When I get down in the barn in the mornings and say "Good morning, Pedro," he whinners as if to answer me, "Good morning, Arnold."

"Pedro" is very fond of apples and we have a big orchard of apples so "Pedro" is going to have all he can eat. I tried to feed him sugar but he just shook his head and spit it out as if to say, "That's too sweet for me." "Pedro" is 44 inches high and weighs 300 pounds.

When I said I was going to win a pony, some of my friends told me it was all a fake and that I wouldn't get anything but I knew that the Webb Publishing Company gave away ponies and I thought I could just as well get a pony as any other boy or girl if I only tried.

There are a good many friends who want to buy "Pedro," but I would not sell him for any price, as I could not live without him. "Pedro" just loves music and whenever my sisters play the piano he feels so contented.

I think every boy and girl should have a pony as it brings happiness to every family and makes them stronger by staying out of doors so much. Many thanks to Webb Publishing Company for my pony "Pedro" and his dandy riding outfit.

A Happy Family

I sure was a happy boy when I got your letter telling me that I had won a pony. I could hardly wait for the day to come when "Bullet" was to arrive. I used to go to the depot every day of the week and when he finally came I was so glad that I did not know what to do.

I took him out of his crate and he was so glad to get out and right there I made a new friend and today he is the best friend and playmate I have in the world.

My papa built a nice barn for him upon the hill back of our house and after he was there a few days he knew his place and it was not necessary for me to lead him in; I just turn him loose and he makes right for his place and he finds his oats there and he sure likes it. When I wake up in the morning and call him by his name which is "Bullet" he looks at me as much as to say "Aren't you going to give me my breakfast" and he will stand there 'till I give him his oats.

He is sure smart; we can teach him almost anything. He shakes hands with me, comes in the kitchen and we give him sugar and then he goes over to the sink and gets his oats. Then I take him

Best Friend (bf)

Shaking Hands

out and saddle him and when we go to town he rides in the stores with me and everybody here thinks he is the "cutest" little pony they ever saw. They all ask me where I got him and I tell them that The Farmer made me a present of him for getting subscribers and a good many of the kids said that they wished they could get one, so I gave them your name and address and told them to write to you and that you would tell them how to get one.

After I had "Bullet" for a while I wanted to know how I could make some money with him so I went to our local News Agent and asked him if I could not sell papers and he told me I could. So the first day I took out ten Denver Posts and he gave me a nice bag to put them in with a strap that fits over my shoulder and I did not have any trouble selling my first ten papers. "Bullet" really sold the papers for me because he is so cute that people would stop and look at him and ask questions about him and then I would ask them if they would not like to buy a paper and I would sell

Playing Stage Coach Robber

one to pretty near everybody that stopped and looked at "Bullet." I would also let the children in town ride him around the block and charge them a nickle a ride and that way I make my expenses of buying his oats and also paid back my Father the money he spent on building his little barn.

Last month I made eight dollars by selling papers and giving children a ride and running errands for our neighbors.

I would not sell "Bullet" for any price as he is the best and dearest friend I have in the world, and if any boy is lucky enough to win a pony I think he is the happiest in the United States.

17

One day as I was looking through a farm paper I saw the pictures of a lot of little Shetland Ponies and boys and girls riding them. I read about them and it said the Webb Publishing Company gave them away to little boys and girls. I asked mamma if I might enter the contest and win one of the ponies. She said I might, so I sent in my application as a contestant.

In a short while I received an answer to my letter and one thousand free votes towards winning one of the ponies. I started out with my sample copy of "The Farmer's Wife" which I had received. I said to mamma as I went out that I was going to get one dozen subscribers that evening. She said "You will do well if you do." I did better than that. Everybody I asked subscribed, except one man. He said there was nothing in it; said I would not fool with that if I were you, it would be some cheap article I would get if I got anything.

So after I won "Princess" and outfit I was out driving and met him and he said, "Hello, that's a nice pony and outfit you are driving, it's the nicest pony in town." Then I told him that was the cheap article he said I would get, and he said, "I declare I did not know they gave such nice ponies and outfits; you

Basket of Flowers (ba)

"Proud of My Pony"

certainly were lucky in winning it," and I think so, too.

I think she was rightly named "Princess" for she is so pretty and smart. She will shake hands with me for sugar and do lots of cute tricks. I could hire her out for fifty cents an hour, but I won't do that, for I am afraid she would be mistreated and I think too much of her to have her mistreated. No princess was ever more proud of her kingdom than I am of my pony "Princess." I went to visit my Grandma this summer and could not take "Princess" along, and I was so anxious to see her that when I came back home I had to go to the barn and see her before I went in the house.

I have three little brothers and two little sisters whom God has taken away, and before I got "Princess" I could not go and take flowers to put on their graves, as it was too far to walk to the cemetery. Now brother and I can drive "Princess" and take flowers and she doesn't seem a bit tired when we get back home.

I wish every boy and girl could have a nice pony like "Princess" and lots of them could if they would only go to work and try to win one, for I am sure the Webb Publishing Company will do what they say they will. I get letters from girls and boys all over the country asking me about my pony, and I tell them she is just a dandy.

"TRIXIE"
FRANK HARRIS, YELLOWSTONE CO., MONTANA

I must let you know how I am getting along with my pony. I couldn't say thanks enough to you for that nice outfit. I have had her hitched up lots of times, and she drives so nice. Nearly everybody comes to see her and they all say what a pretty little outfit I got. She is feeling good; she is not lonesome. She likes oats. When I open the feed box she is scratching and making noise and she always has to get oats the first one.

I wish every little boy or girl owned a nice Sheltie like "Betty" which The Webb Publishing Co. gave me for winning in a Pony Contest. I ride her quite often when the weather is nice. One day I rode her seven miles and back again. She isn't one bit lazy. She walks or trots or gallops just as I want her to. I hitch her up to my nice buggy which they sent with the harness and she drives just as nice and travels real fast. Some of my little friends stay all night with me and we always drive her. They were delighted with her. Lots of them say they are going to try to win a pony.

The train was delayed so "Betty" didn't arrive until Christmas night. My papa and mama began to feel very disappointed and told me I surely did not win, but I told them not to talk like that. I was sure "Betty" and all the outfit would come and they did. We live 16 miles from Beach and papa and I went to meet "Betty" the day after Christmas. All the help at the depot were as pleased as I was and all escorted me to the freight room where "Betty" was uncrated and tied up eating hay. A little friend and I who hauled a load of grain after

Betty's Delight (bd)

"Betty" and Baby Playing Merry-Go-Round

papa's team hauled her home in our wagon and although it was midnight, mamma was waiting and led the pony right into the house. Every few days I ride right into the kitchen and dining room.

"Betty" is a fine little pony. My mother teaches school and we always drive "Betty" to school. When I first saw "Betty" in the depot, I thought she was very small but after I had had her awhile I found she was not as small as I thought she was. When I took her to school she would whinny every little while and the school children would all laugh. When I hitch her up and start off to school she trots along pretty lively. She pulls over five hundred pounds besides the buggy, and trots along very easily. "Betty" likes bread, candy and sugar. She chases our big horses all around the pasture. She is so cute.

I am eleven years old. I have many good times with "Betty." When I call her she will come to me. People have asked me how much I would take for her but I told them she was not for sale. I like to get the cows with her and she likes to chase the cows. I have a pair of chaps and some-

times I play cowboy. All North Dakota boys like to play cowboy. I have a lariat rope and I can rope the cows.

We have another farm six and one-half miles from where we live and my grandmother lives five miles away. One week I made two trips to our other farm and two trips to my grandmother's. Sometimes I ride her to Burkey horseback.

"All North Dakota Boys Like to Play Cowboy"

If she thinks I have feed for her, she will whinny. I have no brothers or sisters. I tried to win a pony before but I did not succeed so I thought I would try again, and sure enough I won "Betty," the best little pony in the country.

I must write and tell you that my little Shetland Pony, "Bud" got here Wednesday afternoon at five o'clock and I was so happy that I could hardly sleep that night and almost forgot to go to school next morning. There were so many people around "Bud" at the railroad station that I thought I never could get him home to our farm. A little later the beautiful buggy and harness and saddle and bridle came too and I surely am proud of the whole outfit.

When I want to go to a picnic, I take my little pony and drive him. He takes the buggy right along as easy as can be and he is as kind as a kitten. I take my pony to town for groceries sometimes and sometimes I take my mamma out for a ride in the afternoon. One day mamma and I went six miles and I thought that "Bud" would be tired but he did not get tired or lazy. My little pony likes to eat apples, sugar and cake and he just loves to drink milk. When I call or whistle for him, he comes up to me and then goes away before I get a chance to catch him, but when I have an apple in my hand, he comes right up to me and seems to ask me for the apple.

"Bud" is so accommodating that he will do anything we ask of him. One day a crowd of us went out on a picnic and

Best of All (be)

"He Ate Right at the Table"

BY SALMA DILLBERG, LYON CO., MINNESOTA

"Bud" acted just like a little boy. When lunch time came, he walked right up to the table and whinnied for his share so we gave him sandwiches and apples and cake and he ate right at the table with us. Then we went out in a nearby field and hitched him up to an old tractor and it was too funny to see him try to pull us along—about a 10 ton load. Of course, he couldn't do it, but he pretended to try, anyway. He seemed to think it was a good joke and didn't fuss a bit. You can see how cute he looks in the two pictures which we took on that day.

When I was trying to get my pony, all my friends said that I would not get it, but I did not listen to that but went right ahead and that is the way all the boys and girls should do when they try to get ponies and every little boy and girl should have a Shetland Pony like mine. "Bud" can jump over a box and he can also do some other cute little tricks. Now, boys and girls, is the time for you to try to get a little Shetland Pony and I know the Webb Publishing Co. will help you to get one because they always do just as they say they will do. All boys and girls should try hard to have a Shetland Pony of their own, and if they get one like "Bud" they will have the best present in the world.

"It Was Too Funny to See Him Try to Pull Us Along"

One very cold Saturday morning in January there came to our house a paper and in it was a row of little Shetland ponies with boys and girls riding on them. There was another picture of a little pony which the Webb Publishing Company was going to give away free. The more I looked at the picture the more I wanted the little pony for my own. My mamma and papa read it and said I might try if I wanted. So I signed my name and mailed it that day and the very day my Certificate of Entry came I began to take subscriptions.

When I first started to get subscriptions, it was pretty hard work, but the more names I got the more I could get and I had lots of pleasant experiences. Some said, "You will not get a pony any way;" others said that I would. I knew the Webb Publishing Company did just as they agreed, for I wrote to some boys and girls who had won ponies and they told me how nice the Webb Publishing Company had been to them. One of the girls I wrote to was Miss Cleta Johnson, who had won "Jerry," and now she and I write to each other about our ponies and the fine times we have with them, so you see the Webb Publishing Company were the means of my making a new friend, for which I thank them very much. I would say to any little boy or girl who is wishing for a pony to enter the Webb Publishing Company's Pony Contest and they will surely win a pony for their own if they only work hard enough.

Broken Heart (bh)

Finally the contest came to a close and then came the anxious days of waiting to know if I had won. Then came my precious letter on Wednesday morning saying that "Tip" would be shipped that week. Saturday night came and no pony. I was most discouraged. Tuesday morning before school my grandpa came down and brought the rest of the outfit which came that morning. Then I felt sure that my pony would soon be here. Wednesday night after school, I got a telephone message that my pony was at the station and maybe we did not hustle down after him.

When I saw him my joy knew no bounds. I put my arms around his neck and said, "Oh, you little darling." How I did hug him, I was so glad he had come and was mine. He did not like his ride on the cars at all, for he had ridden 47 hours. "Tip" had kicked himself completely out of his crate and they had to put him in the freight house. We live four miles from the station and I thought we would never get home, for everyone came out to see my pony, for "Tip" is the first pony owned in our town. One lady said she just wanted to touch him; I suppose to see if he really was alive.

continued on next page

"'Tip' and the Whole Family Enjoy Reading The Farmer's Wife"

continued

We brought him home and turned him loose in a nice box stall we had made on purpose for him. "Tip" was Oh, so hungry and tired. He would eat a little then lie down; then get up and eat some more, then lie down. The next day he seemed rested some so I put on his saddle and bridle and rode him a little. "Tip" is just as gentle as he can be.

"Tip" will follow me all over with no halter on. He will come up the steps onto the porch into the house and look out of the windows. I have a big bull-dog named "Sport" and he will hold "Tip's" halter rope so "Tip" can eat grass on the lawn. "Tip" dearly loves apples and will take them out of my pocket. He will shake hands and do many cute things, but of all the children that play with him, he seems to like me best. He does not like strangers at all. I draw wood for mamma and take eggs to town for groceries for her and mamma pays me for all I do, so you see "Tip" is making me rich.

I cannot begin to tell you all the good times I have had since "Tip" came to live with me. I have always been sickly but now I play with "Tip" so much out of doors that I am getting strong and well. I have had lots of chances to sell "Tip," but money cannot buy him, for my heart would be broken if I ever had to part with him. And I know "Tip's" would be too for we are such friends. We all like The Farmer's Wife very much and "Tip" and the whole family enjoy reading it.

Indian on Horseback (in)

I give "Tip" a bath real often and braid his mane and tail to make him look nice. He likes to be curried and fussed with. When winter comes I am going to have a new sled to hitch "Tip" to, then we will have jolly times in the snow. So you see "Tip" is making me very happy, also my little friends.

If all little boys and girls could only have a pony like my "Tip," I am sure they would all love it as dearly as I do "Tip" and have as many good times as I do. I am sure they would be very

26

much happier. Since "Tip" came to live with me I have had company nearly every day and all the children love "Tip" most as much as I do for I let them all ride him, but I am sure "Tip" likes me best of all.

I can never thank The Farmer's Wife enough for sending "Tip" to me.

"Tip" at a Lawn Party

"Freckles"
Dorothy Biebighauser, Washington Co., Minnesota

"Freckles" reached us the 10th, and I think he is the dearest little pony I ever saw. My little brother and I are the happiest children on earth. We put him in our orchard, and we can go in any time and catch him. Yesterday we played around him all day.

He is so gentle, we wonder how old he is. My brother is six years old and I am eight. One of us sits on him and the other leads him, that's the way we take rides.

Mamma will take our picture soon then we will send it to you.

One Saturday morning, free from our school duties, we boys sat down to look over a farm paper. Nothing of note attracted our attention until we turned a page and there stood the cutest little pony all hitched to a cart, with the words: "Free to Some Lucky Boy or Girl." Greatly excited over the prospect of having such a dandy little rig, we ran to mother who carefully read and explained the matter to us. We thought we could win it or at least we would try very hard, so mother gave us her consent and we sent a card for full directions for beginning.

In a few days, we received the directions and got Mother for the first subscriber. Then our work began in earnest. Some days we got quite a number and some days only a few. We had no trouble in getting people to take the paper for they knew it to be valuable. Sometimes, we were discouraged, but we remembered that one boy and one girl in our own county had won a pony and buggy and we worked harder than ever.

We waited in great suspense for the returns of the contest and when they came, we were almost afraid to open the letter for fear we

***Boy's Playmate* (bp)**

The Twins Are Tickled Over "Empress"

28

had not won. But what was our joy when upon opening it, Avery and Orie Knight led the list. The letter said that "Empress," would arrive in a few days.

One morning a few days afterward, while eating our breakfast, a man yelled, "Come out here and take care of your horse." My what a stampede! We all ran out doors and the express man was just coming into the yard. When he unloaded there was the sweetest little black pony with a white halter. No breakfast food for us that morning.

The first thing we wanted to do was to ride her up town, but Father said she was tired after her long ride, so we put her in the barn and gave her some hay. Oh, what a long day that

was with our dear little pony in the barn and we unable to ride her! But the next day finally came and we were up bright and early and rode her up town. Everybody was nearly as tickled over her as we were. That morning before school, it seemed as if half the town was down there admiring her.

When hitched to the buggy, "Empress," looks like a dear little rabbit traveling along shaking its head.

She comes in the house and eats from the table and acts like a real little lady. When we ride her any place and leave her standing outside by the porch, she comes up the steps and tries to get in. She grew to love us during our long vacation and when school began again she would whinner when she heard Mother come out of doors, as if asking for her little friends.

We drive "Empress" to town after groceries for Mother and we drive her to Sunday School nearly every Sunday. Our little brother likes to feed our other pets, such as doves, and bantam chickens, but he likes nothing better than to share his cookies and apples with "Empress."

"Brother Likes to Share His Apples With 'Empress'"

Last spring out to sunny Kansas from his home away up North in the cold country, came my darling little pony, "Sunny Jim." His eyes were just like little tiny suns and everyone who sees him, their eyes shine too and mamma says he is a regular little ball of sunshine out in sunny Kansas for a little sunny girl and his name is "Sunny Jim."

When I was a little tiny girl my grandpa said, "Some day I'll buy you a nice little Shetland pony." Once when I was sick and the doctor's medicine was very bitter he said, "Just take it, dearie, and go to sleep and some day when you wake up the Shetland pony will be here." I always dreamed of little Shetlands all black and spotted but they always ran away when I woke up. Now my grandpa is a real nice baldheaded grandpa and when I was a baby they called me a boy's name just because his name was Joe. So I thought if all my life I had to be called a boy's name he ought to buy me a pony. But my auntie said when she was a little girl grandpa told her the very same thing and now she is too big to ride and would never know what good times she had missed. So I just knew my grandpa was having dreams too, when he promised to buy me one. But one day my dream came true and I'm going to tell you how.

One day a paper came to our house and the first thing I found in that paper was a whole page of little Shetland ponies and boys and girls riding on them. I read about it and it said the

Bright Hopes (br)

Webb Publishing Company of St. Paul, gave them away to little boys and girls. My mamma read it too and she said if I wanted to I might enter the contest. I was awful bashful and didn't like to go to people's houses, but mamma said, "Just take the sample copy of the paper with you and you won't have any trouble getting people to subscribe." I just went to ladies' houses I knew at first and they said of course we will take your paper and I told them I would take their little children out riding when I got my pony. I got so many right at first that I got real brave and would go to nearly anyone's house after school and just ask everyone I met.

Some man would say, "You bet I'll take your paper," and then he would say, "Hey Bill and John, come and help this little girl out." Sometimes Bill and John would say, "Oh, there isn't anything to it. My boy sold something to get a kite and he never heard from the place again." I wasn't afraid to say things when they thought the Webb Publishing Company would do that way, for I knew better than that. And I had lots of letters from little girls who had got ponies.

Sometimes a woman said, "We just don't see how we can take it, we get so many papers now and the children have had the measles and all the bills coming in." But I just kept right on showing her the little pictures of the pony and turning the pages of the magazine till pretty soon she would look a little nicer and say, "I always wished my little girl could have a pony." Then she would just say, "I'll take it," and when I left she would be smiling real pretty and looking nearly young enough to ride a pony, and I knew my little pony was making people happy even before it came to live in our town.

continued on next page

"Two of My Dearest Friends"

continued

I know lots of men who work on the road near my house and they all took my paper, because they had chickens and gardens and cows. But I believe the real reason was that some time in their lives they had had a grandpa who said, "Some day I'll buy you a pony," and it never came, just like the dreams I had when I was sick and the doctor came.

When I got the letter from the Webb Publishing Company telling me that I had won the prize I was so glad I nearly cried. I made my grandpa sit up and take me to the train that night. The first night I went to meet him the pony didn't come as his train was delayed. So we all went to meet him the next night and sure enough he was there and the baggage man helped me up in the car and I was so happy I forgot to scold "Jim" for being a day late. I never said a bad word to him because he just looked up with his little sparkling eyes and he knew me from everybody else who came to see him and he just squealed the cutest little squeal and stuck his ears up and rubbed his wet nose all over my coat. Everybody wanted him to look at them but he just knew it was me he had come to live with, and when the depot man helped grandpa take him out of his box "Sunny Jim" let me get right on his back and grandpa led him up through Main Street, everybody coming along behind him.

After every one had gone home and it was nearly morning time we put him in a little lot by

Summer's Dream (sd)

the barn. He was so glad to have a nice home and acted so cute I could hardly say goodnight to him. But early before school the next morning I was to see him again and after school all the little boys and girls came to see him and we had a big party and little "Sunny" was the guest of honor just like they have big folks' parties.

Every little boy and girl in town loves "Sunny Jim" because he is the only little pony in town and I take them all driving after school in my little buggy. When winter comes I am going to have a little sled and then we will all have a jolly time in the snow.

"Jim" will eat anything I give him. He loves sugar, bananas and candy and it makes him too fat for he weighs 50 pounds more now than he did when he came. He will come up the steps on the porch and he will turn on the hydrant in the yard when he wants a drink. And he does the most cute things.

My mamma took me to visit in the mountains this summer and she wouldn't take "Sunny Jim" along so I couldn't stay very long as I got too homesick to see him and I coaxed her to come home pretty soon. One of my little chums kept him for me while I was gone.

"Jim" gets me scolded lots of times but he doesn't know he's doing wrong. Every time I wear a nice clean dress my mamma says, "What makes those black streaks on your dress?" She doesn't know, but "Jim" does. He just rubs his nice little dusty nose all over my back. I don't care, because dresses wash, and dear little "Jim" just does it because he loves me so.

I love the Webb Publishing Company more than anything in the world except "Sunny Jim," because if the man that published the paper hadn't loved us little girls and boys so much I would never have won my own darling "Sunny Jim" and my dream would never have come true.

"'Sunny Jim' Knew Me From Everybody Else Who Came to Meet Him"

My name is Edwin Larson. I am ten years old and I live in Worcester County, Mass. I won a pony named "Early Bird" from the Webb Publishing Company, and he's the cutest little pony I ever saw. He is 41 inches high, but he will grow some more, for he is only two years and six months old. I can drive him anywhere. He isn't afraid of anything and he is as strong as a horse. He can pull me and my two brothers and two sisters in his little cart no matter how far we want to go, and how he can run. I think he can run faster than some big horses. One day when I was out for a drive I met a man driving and he asked me if I wanted to go on a race and I said yes. He got so far behind that I couldn't see him. My "Early Bird" can run like a deer and a good many of my chums would like to have him, but I won't sell him for ever so much money. I have lots of fun with my pony and I wish every boy and girl could get one. They don't cost much to keep because they don't eat much.

I think "Early Bird" is a good name for my pony for I can take him out very early in the morning for a drive. He is always ready no matter how early it is. My father and mother have been out for a good many early rides this summer and they like my pony just as much as I do. When we had this picture taken we had just been out for a ride. Mamma always comes out and pets the pony when we get home, for she likes him so much.

Bird's Eye View (bv)

My pony likes apples and sugar. One day I had an apple inside of my blouse. I was going to fool him and not give it to him, but he chased me all over the yard till he got me into a corner. There he unbuttoned my blouse and took the apple.

One day last winter I took an apple and buried it in the snow and I told him I had an apple for him and pointed out where it was and he started digging in the snow till he found

34

it. He is awfully fond of snow. He likes to play in it, same as I do. We had lots of snow here last winter so I had lots of sleigh rides with my "Early Bird" and I hope I get some more next winter because its lots of fun. One day last winter I let him out all alone. He started to run away from home. I was afraid he was going to get lost so I opened the door and called him and he came right back and jumped right up on the piazza where I stood. Then I gave him a piece of sugar and he was all right.

I hope the Webb Publishing Company will give away lots of more ponies to girls and boys for I think they are the nicest pets anybody can have.

"Mamma Always Pets 'Early Bird' When We Get Home"

I always thought I wanted to own a pony, so one day last Spring about the first of February, I saw in the paper that the Webb Publishing Company was giving away ponies and I wanted them to give me one. I knew I could have one just as well as not if I worked hard enough, because one of my little friends, Roy Brown, of McCook County, South Dakota, won a pony of the Webb Publishing Company and I knew if he did I could. I had seen his pony and he was awful cute, a real live Shetland pony.

The first thing I did was to send in $1.00 with two yearly subscriptions and they sent me my Certificate of Entry and I went to work in earnest. I worked hard every day I could. One man told me I would not get any pony. He said if I did he would give me 50 cents, but I haven't seen him since. Some day I will drive over and let him see "Carlo." He took the paper anyway so that helped some. And nearly everyone took my paper, so finally the 23rd of May the Postmaster phoned us there was a letter for me from the Webb Publishing Company. So mamma went and got it and such news! I had won "Carlo." Before mamma got home all the neighbors and everyone in town knew I had won "Carlo." How happy I was! But I was still more happy when the depot agent phoned out and said our pony was there. That was May 29th. Mamma, papa and ever so many more people met him at the train, and

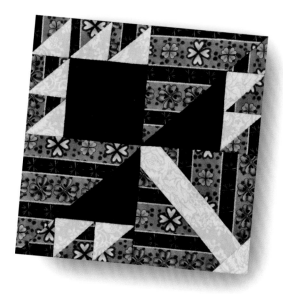

Clover Blossom (cb)

such times as "Carlo" and I and my little sisters, Bessie and Viola, have had ever since.

We go to town after groceries and we are sorry school is out, it would be so nice to drive to school. He likes to eat clover blossoms out of my hat and the girls' aprons.

A short time after we got "Carlo" and he wasn't accustomed to being away from the

"Carlo," Harold and His Two Sisters

other ponies, we left him loose in the yard at night and he started back to the pony farm. Uncle John found him 13 miles from home the next morning, so you see he is some traveler. We went to a circus the other day. My, but "Carlo" did feel proud, because he was just as nice as any pony in the circus and I know he could learn just as many tricks. He will shake hands and when he gets all the water he wants, he will upset the bucket with his foot.

continued on next page

"Now I am Out of Doors All the Time"
Clarence F. Busick, Adams Co., Indiana

How "Roine" Played Doctor

The day I received word that I had won a pony it seemed to me as tho I could not wait until he would arrive. I was sick at the time and could not go and see him. When the doctor heard that I had won a pony, he said that was one of the finest things that I could have for my condition, to be out of doors all the time.

continued

Last Saturday, mamma, Viola, Bessie and I went 10 miles to grandma's and back Sunday and it didn't take us very long to make the trip. The first time we hitched him to his little buggy, we drove to Aunt Maud's and she thought he was the nicest pony she ever saw. He looks so cute with his harness on, and his buggy is the best money can buy. He likes to come in the house or on the porch and try to eat my toes and the other day he tried to unbutton mamma's shoe. One day when mamma was brushing him he reached around and bit her but she just laughed because it didn't hurt one bit.

We want to decorate the buggy and harness, but not "Carlo;" he doesn't need it, and be in the parade the Fourth. We know he would take the prize. He isn't afraid of autos or motorcycles. When anyone sees us together they stop and look and say, "What a cute outfit."

One day two boys on bicycles came 10 miles to see "Carlo." One of the boys was in the contest too, but poor fellow, didn't get votes enough. I know he felt bad about it, but he got a nice rifle anyway.

My parents are glad I won "Carlo" and so are all of my friends. Yesterday I gave Uncle Bert a ride in my buggy and Uncle Dannie a horseback ride. The day the club met at home I gave all of them a ride but Grandpa, and he said he was too fat, but "Carlo" wouldn't care. They liked the ride very much. I wouldn't part with "Carlo"

Maud's Album Quilt (mq)

for any money. Every boy and girl should own a pony as it makes them so healthy to be out of doors so much and I cannot stay in when "Carlo" is out. I know he would get lonesome for me.

Papa is going to roach his mane. Won't he look stylish though? And he will be cooler too. My, but he was proud the day he had his picture taken, just like he knew all about it. We have a white dog named "Smarty;" every place "Carlo" goes "Smarty" has to go. I guess he thinks we are all little and all belong together.

Grandma and Grandpa Gachring think "Carlo" is the nicest pony in the world. Grandpa Bush has not seen him yet, he is up to Uncle Mart's, but he is anxious to get home just to see "Carlo" and his nice outfit.

When I call "Carlo" he sticks up his ears and looks around for me; thinks I am playing hide and seek, I guess. "Carlo" loves to go with me after water or eggs or to feed the little chicks. His feet are very tiny and he makes such cute little tracks. Papa says "Carlo" has better feet than lots of big horses and he trots awfully cute. I am very proud of him and his outfit and I thank the Webb Publishing Company again for "Carlo." I could write more because every day is just like a circus since I got "Carlo." I hope every boy and girl that wants one will work and get it of the Webb Publishing Company because theirs are the best.

"Carlo" Is a Member of the Bush Family

One evening while looking at one of Papa's farm papers, I found a picture of a pony hitched to a wagon with boys and girls in it. I spoke to mamma about it but she did not pay any attention to me at first, but I kept talking to mamma and papa both about it till they said I could write to The Farmer's Wife and see what I had to do to get a pony.

Then I went right to work as soon as I heard from them, getting subscriptions. It was about the middle of the contest before I began, so papa helped me. We got subscribers every day and it did not seem long before the last day came. When we were getting subscribers some people said I would just get a picture of a pony, but we kept right on. Papa and mamma thought I would get a pony but I did not.

At last I got a letter from them saying I had won a pony and her name was "Dainty." Then I waited and waited but I heard nothing more from them till one night when we were eating supper the telephone rang and mamma answered it. It was the express man. I heard them say something about a pony and I could not keep still till they stopped talking. Then we hurried and went down to the station about a mile from our house. Mamma and I drove one horse on the carriage and papa drove the other horse on the one-horse wagon. When we came back I rode with papa and "Dainty." Everybody was saying, "Oh! Look at the cute little pony they just got at the station."

Colt's Corral (cc)

When we got home we took her out of her crate and I led her around. That night was the first time I ever saw her trot and I hollered to mamma to look at her. I was so surprised and she looked so cute.

She was not large enough for me to ride her much at first because she was a little "Special Pony," but she soon got bigger. I like to ride her and do almost every day. Then I always give her something good for her pay.

I do not go to school in our district as there are not enough children to pay for hiring a teacher, so a man is hired to carry us to the next school-house. It is two and one-half miles from my home and sometimes I ride "Dainty." Papa had a little sleigh made for "Dainty" and I am going to have a harness. Next winter I expect to drive to St. Albans to see my aunt. I have ridden "Dainty" nearly seven miles at one time and she wasn't tired.

"Dainty" likes almost everything to eat but milk, cream, butter and meat. She loves ripe apples but will not eat green ones. In winter I always give her grain, but in the summer she is in the pasture or meadow so I don't give it to her very much.

continued on next page

We Hauled "Dainty" Home in the One Horse Wagon

continued

When "Dainty" meets an auto she hardly looks at it. She is not afraid of anything.

I would not sell "Dainty" for any money. I would not know what to do without her. All of my friends, big and little, say she is the prettiest pony they ever saw. In the winter "Dainty" looks a lot bigger with her long hair and papa says he believes she is half sheep, she is so woolly.

Mamma and papa think it is awful nice that I have got "Dainty." I had no one to play with before "Dainty" came, but now I have lots of fun.

I took "Dainty" to the Franklin County Fair in September and she won the first prize as a saddle pony. I was very proud of her. You can see her with the blue ribbon on in one picture.

"Dainty" learns very easy. She can do quite a number of tricks. She will shake hands, kiss me, stand her fore feet on papa's or my knees, come in the house and eat off from the table if she gets a chance, and stand with her fore feet on a box, chair or steps. She will let me slide down her back when her fore feet are higher than her hind feet.

We used to let "Dainty" run about in the door yard, but this summer up at the next farm there were two little colts and "Dainty" thought they were ponies. She would go right up there where they were and look at them, so we had to put her in the pasture. Once when I was riding "Dainty" we met another little pony

Cat's Paw (cp)

and "Dainty" almost stopped to look at it, but I guess "Dainty" is glad she isn't that pony for they were whipping it and making it go just as fast as it could.

My little black kitten likes to have me take him on "Dainty's" back when I am riding her. Sometimes I put him on her in the pasture and he will rough up her hair with his paw and then lick it down again.

One night I went after the cows and when I got down in the pasture where the cows were, I went up to "Dainty" and got right on her back with no saddle or even a bridle on her and rode her up back of the cows, and she came just as nice.

When I got "Dainty" she weighed only 195 pounds, but now she weighs 308 pounds. She is just as fat as butter. She can hardly get in the crate she came in so the pictures do not look the same as when I got her.

I think, when the Webb Publishing Company gives away ponies for so little work and such nice ponies too, that every little boy and girl should have a pony and I wish they could. I can't thank the Webb Publishing Company enough for giving me "Dainty."

"Dainty" Winner of the Blue Ribbon

"CUSTER"
GIVEN TO LEE MOHR, MARSHALL CO., IOWA

Lee has fine times driving "Custer" in his little home made Brake Cart.

One day while looking over a farm paper I saw a page of Shetland Ponies and thought I would try to win one of them, so the next day I sent in the Certificate of Entry. As I was getting subscribers one day, I met a man and I asked him if he wanted to subscribe and he said "yes." Then I told him I was going to try to win a pony and he said, "Oh! that's it." Then he said, "Gitdap! Gitdap!" and let me stand there, but it only made me laugh. I thought he was pretty stingy. I met several like that but I didn't care.

When the contest closed I was anxious to hear who had won "Inez." One day I got a letter that I had won "Inez." I jumped way up and my sister asked me if I was getting a little crazy, and I hollered, "Oh! Marie, the pony has come." And my little sister, Pearl said, "Oh! goody goody!" I called up lots of children and in the morning when I came to school I was very happy. I have very much fun with my dear little pony, "Inez."

"Inez" is a beautiful pony, so cute and so smart. She is 40 inches high and weighs about 350 pounds. I love her dearly and for fun, she is the best chum I have. I have a cat and two dogs but none as good as "Inez." She eats ice cream and all good things. She goes on our big porch and is the pet of all the neighbors. In the summer she comes up to the house and begs for something to eat. Last summer my little sister was eating her breakfast and "Inez" came

Children's Delight (cd)

up to her and begged it away from her.

One day I thought I would make a sled, so I took one of papa's old sleds apart and made some shafts and it looked pretty good. I also drive her around a lot in a little express wagon on which I put some shafts. This is probably the smallest express outfit in the state. "Inez" always likes to be out. Last summer we used to lead her all around the yard. I hope all you

44

children who are trying hard to win a pony, will get one. Everybody said, "Oh, you will get a wooden pony or else a rocking horse." My teacher's sister said her little cousin was trying to get a pony too, but he never heard of the Company any more. Then I said, "There aren't very many Companies that are as true as the Webb Publishing Company either." Everybody laughed at me but I didn't care, I let them laugh just as much as they wanted to, and I laugh now. When they saw they couldn't get me discouraged, they took the paper.

"Smallest Express Outfit in the State"

Dapple in coming way over 1,000 miles to his new home, traveled farther than most of the other prize ponies given by the Webb Publishing Company. He came East to within a few miles of the great Atlantic Ocean, and now lives in southeastern Pennsylvania, that land of fine farms and fancy horses and even here he is considered a winner. He, and two others, out of more than 100 ponies given by the Webb Publishing Company have come to this great state.

A wide state road connects our country place with quite a large town. Along this road "Dapple" and I speed with my little friends. The horsemen in this neighborhood know "Dapple" well and like him particularly for his fine trotting action. We believe him to be the fastest as well as the prettiest pony in this section. He is a fine silky chestnut, rather dark with faint dapples showing through—a beautiful mane and tail reaching to the ground—a fine head and a proud arched neck. "Dapple" likes me to talk to him, softly, with my head against his and he answers me with his nose. You never saw an animal that likes to have his face and head washed and rubbed as much as "Dapple" does.

I am going to show him at the Horse Fair and have him in the races at the great York County Fair this fall, and "Dapple" will win I am sure. He walks so proudly, just

County Fair (cf)

Feeding "Dapple" Grass

as though he measures each step with his cunning little foreleg.

You will notice "Dapple" and his dandy cart decorated for the Memorial Day parade held in our city the very next month after I won him. He acted splendidly, as though he came from a family of acting horses and I had him but a few weeks. "Dapple" will be in the Fourth of July parade too.

Listen to the contest. It was more than half over when I started. I had never heard of the Webb Publishing Company until my uncle [my father's little brother] received a rifle for selling a magazine. In that magazine was "Dapple's" picture advertised and "Dapple" asking, "Do You Want Me?" I did, and started getting subscriptions. At first it was hard work but after you know "The Farmer's Wife" and its Publishing House, you become enthusiastic. Don't get discouraged. If you want a pony like I did, you must want it hard enough to win, and to win the first prize in the Webb Publishing Company Contests (the pony, cart, bridle, saddle, harness and expressage to your home) you must stand first and there is but one first. You must beat the other boys and girls and they are working just like you. When ladies say, "It's no use, they'll give no pony," just show them a copy of "Lucky Pony Winners." It will convince them that real live ponies are given away, and that you are going to win this one providing she and others give you a subscription to "The Farmer's Wife."

"All Decorated for the Memorial Day Parade"

Will I ever forget the day I got my pony? Oh no, not I. Nor do I think any of our family will, nor will some of those who were working at our place that day. What a joyous day! Some who seldom smiled caught the contagion and joined in the happiness over the pony.

That morning I went over to our little station with papa to ship the cream and I saw my pony in the baggage car. Papa said my eyes will never be bigger. We were not certain he would be on that train but I knew he was mine the minute my eyes saw him. He could not be taken off there as there was no express office there. So the train went on to Proctor, a mile below our place. I watched that train as far as I could see it, for it had that precious pony aboard.

When we got home we ran to tell mamma the pony was on the train. The news was soon spread over the farm and everybody was shouting, "The pony was on the down train."

My papa had a man to watch for the pony and bring him up when he came. So papa telephoned and the answer came he was bringing my "Christy," which is the pony's name. Many glances were cast down the road before we finally saw the pony coming.

"He is coming," my papa shouted. "Come on, boys, out to the road to see the pony." The threshing machine was stopped and thirty-two men lined up to give the pony a royal welcome. He must have enjoyed it for he seemed excited. After he passed through the line, all said, "He'll

Country Lanes (cl)

take the ribbon at any fair." He was examined and examined over again and the more we inspected him, the better we liked him. At last papa says, "Where are you going to put him, C. P.?" And I said, "I just want to hold him." And I held him and led him around by the rope and what do you think? When the mail carrier came, he brought the bridle and saddle. We put them on him and he looked finer than ever. I must have a ride and mamma and the women came out to see me on the pony's back and, I guessed, also to see that I would not get hurt. Papa led "Christy" around a little with me on and I led him around the rest of the day.

I feel so big and important when I let the other boys have a ride. I try not to be selfish and I have fun seeing the others so happy when they ride. I can call him or just whistle and he will run right to me. Of course, he likes me better than all the others. I often have sugar or a banana for him and he likes oats, I tell you. I am going to ride to school on him this winter.

My mamma and papa are glad I got the pony for I am not so slow any more. I can even dress quicker in the mornings for I want to see the pony and I hurry up with the chores so as to get through and have time with the pony. And then I like to work a little, too, for you see I want my pony to have a good home and you have to work to have anything. Then the pony can help. He takes me flying on errands.

I wish every boy and girl every place could have a pony, in the city as well as in the country.

Back From a Ride

"JUDGE"

I live in Morton County, North Dakota. One day when I was looking through the paper for the Young Folks' Page, I found the advertisement, "Do you want a pony free?" So I wrote to the Pony Editor and asked him what I had to do in order to get the pony. He wrote and told me and I started out to work and asked every person I met to subscribe. Many told me that they didn't believe that the Webb Publishing Company gave Shetland ponies away, but I knew better and kept on working as hard as I could until the contest closed.

After the contest closed I could hardly wait to hear from the Company. Finally the good news came that I had won "Judge," and I don't believe there was a happier boy in the United States than I was. I could hardly wait until "Judge" came, and I was so anxious to see him that I couldn't sleep nights. At last on May 28th the saddle and bridle came and on Decoration Day the buggy came. In the forenoon papa set up the buggy and at two o'clock "Judge" was hitched up ready to take a drive. I felt as proud as a king and "Judge" walked along with his head held high and everybody looked at my pony and spoke about how pretty he was.

Cowboy's Star (co)

"I Like to Play Cowboy"

50

"Judge" is the prettiest of all the Shetland ponies in our neighborhood, and I am proud of being the owner of him. "Judge" isn't afraid of engines, autos or anything. When I go to town, I can drive up and down and he is as gentle as a kitten. He just loves apples, candy, sugar and cake and follows me all over the yard and even up the steps and into the kitchen for lump sugar. He can also do a great many tricks. He lies down like a dead horse, shakes hands and tells me how old he is by pawing three times.

I get the milk cows every morning and evening from the pasture with "Judge" and help my papa drive cattle to town when he sells them. "Judge" acts just as though he were a born "cow pony." He keeps them moving all the time and if one breaks away from the bunch "Judge" is after him like a flash and heads him off before he has gone any distance. "Judge" probably saw very few cattle before he came out here, but he is so smart that he learned how to drive them in no time.

Like all Western boys, I like to play cowboy, and I have a dandy cowboy suit that I wear. I ride "Judge" around and lasso cattle just like real cow punchers do, and also chase imaginary Indians all around the plains.

I thank the Webb Publishing Company very much for "Judge" and his beautiful outfit, and I am proud to say that they do all that they promise to do.

"I Get the Milk Cows From the Pasture With 'Judge'"

I was eight years old when I entered the contest in 1910, and my sister was three years old. We were so sad and lonesome then until "Bob" came to live with us, for my papa is away from home so much and our dear mamma passed away on October 18, 1909. While my sister and I are on our way to Sunday School driving "Bob" I think I can see mamma watching us up in heaven, and I hope to meet all the pony winners together with the Webb Publishing Company in heaven and if there is a heaven for ponies I know "Bob" will go for he is so good. The Webb Publishing Company is so very good and kind to make my sister and me so happy by sending such a nice good pony and outfit.

Papa and all of the neighbors love "Bob" also and say so many good things about the Webb Publishing Company, for they are sure friends to boys and girls who will work for a pony. If you win the next pony contest you will be the happiest boy or girl in the world.

I would like to have all the pony winners come to Arkansas to visit "Bob" and me. We have plenty of room and water, also a little Barley Corn. You see John Barley Corn, Jr., is my name, I was named for papa. My papa was born in Lincoln County, Tennessee, where they made barley corn famous. Grandpa liked barley corn so well and his name being Corn he decided to call papa John Barley Corn. Then I arrived and papa named me John Barley Corn, Jr. My sister, who was born on the first day of June, is called

Confederate Rose (cr)

Bessie June Corn, so you see "Bob" has June and Barley Corn all the time and do you wonder he is so good?

When I grow up to be a man I expect to run for governor of Arkansas on the Prohibition ticket and show people that John Barley Corn is good for something besides ruining homes.

Now, don't you hesitate to enter the next contest and put confidence in the Webb Publishing Company for they will do all they say. I just cannot tell you how much I love them for what they did for my sister and me.

continued on page 54

The Farmer's Wife Pony Club Contest

In reply to Mabel Erdley's request to become a Pony Club member, she was sent a letter and instructions on how to enter *The Farmer's Wife* magazine subscription contest. The club rules were few, but the most important was that she not spend her own money to pay for subscriptions for other people. For, as the editors explained to Mabel, "This makes our club competition fair to rich and poor alike because our ponies will go to boys and girls who HUSTLE and get subscribers and NOT to children who have rich parents who would be willing to spend a lot of money to give away subscriptions to win."

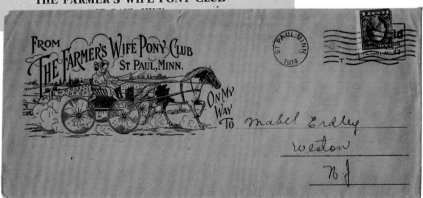

continued

"Bob" is a beautiful pony, so cute and smart. He is forty-one inches high and weighs three hundred pounds. He loves me dearly and for fun he is the best chum I have. He is very fond of eating sugar and I taught him to do so many cute things, for he learns so very easy. He will lie down and play asleep, shake hands, nod for yes, and shake his head for no, he will walk on his hind feet, kneel and say his prayers. In the morning when he awakes he always nickers for me. I enjoy so much driving in the country with my friends to get watermelons and peaches.

This spring my little sister and I drove "Bob" in the National Confederate Reunion Parade. The buggy and pony looked so pretty decorated. We were also in the Labor Day Parade this year and "Bob" won the prize of a new bridle for being the prettiest and smallest pony in the parade. There were also other boys in the parade with their ponies. The new bridle looks just fine on "Bob" and he is so very proud of it.

During school days I drive "Bob" to

Fishing Boats (fb)

"Bob" Is Ready for the Parade

54

school and on Sunday morning I take my little sister to Sunday School.

"Bob" and I are always glad when papa takes us along on a fishing trip. I go in swimming and "Bob" likes to swim also, he can swim with me on his back. I have a canvas boat that I get into and hold to "Bob's" tail while he pulls me across the river, which is about fifty yards across. When we are through fishing papa loads up the buggy with fish and we start home. I hope all the lucky winners live near a river so they can take their pony for a swim. At first your pony will not like it but he soon learns it is fine sport.

I have a bull dog, whom you can see in the picture; he and "Bob" are great chums. They sleep together and wherever "Bob" goes the dog is sure to go, just like Mary's Little Lamb. One day "Bob" got away and was gone all day, but my dog followed and drove him home safely just in time for his sugar and a nice supper which I had ready for him.

I have been offered $300.00 for "Bob" but I would not sell him for any price, for I have more pleasure out of my pony and buggy than to have so much money and no pony. My dog and I would be so lonesome without "Bob." I know he would cry much if taken away.

"Bob" Is So Cute and Smart

My Pony "Nipper"

Nipper is a lovely pony, so gentle and kind. He is a bay, 38 ½ inches high, and weighs 290 pounds. He knows when I have a piece of cake and will whinny for some and follow me all over until I give him some and if I don't give it to him he will come up and put his head over my shoulder and coax for some. He does this too cute for anything and we like to see him do it so much that we make him coax often. He is also fond of cake, pretzels and candy. When he gets thirsty he will come up to the door and ask for a drink by whinnying.

Every day I take him for a drive and take my little brother with me and when my brother is asleep I give my playmates a ride. I have so many playmates that are always ready to go with me that I have to give each one a turn. Papa made me a little truck wagon and I go to the store for mamma and to the mill for "Nipper's" feed and he knows when I go to mill, for on his way home I can hardly hold him, and as soon as he is unharnessed he is nosing around the feed bag.

Cake Stand (cs)

"Coaxing for Cake"

"Nipper" is admired by everyone along the road. These are some of the remarks I hear, "Isn't he cute." "My! What a beautiful pony." "He is too cute to be driven," and many other sayings. He has a beautiful tail and mane. When papa gets up in the morning he takes "Nipper" over in the grass patch where he is always ready to go. When I get up I clean his stable and then I bring him from the grass patch and give him a good cleaning. Then he gets his breakfast.

I only had "Nipper" about a month when a man came to papa and wanted to know how much papa would take for him. Papa said he did not own him and that he should ask me and I told him I wouldn't sell him for any money. My cousin is so fond of him that his father is going to buy him one and when he gets his we will have great times together.

There are so many more things that I could write about him, but it would take me all day to write of all the pleasures I have had since I have my pony. I value him more than anything I have or ever had, and I cannot thank the Webb Publishing Company enough for giving me a chance to win such a pony as "Nipper."

"Off to the Store for Mamma"

I *live in Mountrail Co., N. D.,* only about 70 miles from the Montana State line. One day as I was looking over the pages of the paper, I saw several pictures of a lot of boys and girls who had won ponies. It made me long for one so much, so I at once sent in my name and got a Certificate of Entry, and I started the day I got it to take subscriptions.

I was very happy the day I received the news of winning "Captain" and the outfit. I told my friends about it and they were also delighted over it. So many of our neighbors told me the contest would be a fake.

The night "Captain" came pretty near everybody in town was over to the station to meet him. I had received the saddle and riding bridle the day before he came, so I rode him over to town that night and a crowd of boys and girls followed me, they were all so happy. I was even happier myself. I cannot express my joy in words hardly, I was so delighted.

My folks were so pleased when I got "Captain" because they thought I would grow stronger out doors nearly all my time, and I herd my cows every night and morning. I don't think I could ever part with "Captain" he has become so attached to me since I got him, and I hope we shall never have to part from each other.

One day in July there was a picnic near the river, about three miles from home. Gladys, Ruth, Marie, Francis and I decided we would all go to it. So early in the morning I got up and hurried

Captain's Wheel (cw)

out to the barn to feed "Captain" his breakfast as usual, and to talk to him while he was eating, for he likes to have me do so. Then I went out and got "Captain's" chum, "Queen" (a large St. Bernard dog), and brought her in to say "Good Morning" to him as they are the best of friends and very fond of each other. Then I harnessed "Captain" and hitched him up to the buggy, and we started on our way.

First they had a ball game and then the manager of the picnic grounds asked me to show the crowd the tricks "Captain" could do. I sent my brother Francis over to the buggy to untie "Captain," then I whistled for him and he came over to me. He stood up on a box, lay down, shook hands, played hide-and-go-seek, and did many other tricks, for which I received three dollars, the first money I had ever earned with "Captain." I felt proud to think I owned a pony that was so smart.

It was now dinner time. I took "Captain" over to the buggy again and fed him his dinner and we all went over to the grove

"Captain" Likes to Hear Me Play

and ate our lunch, then we went over to the race track and watched the horse races and also foot races. After that we played games. After we had all had our dinner the manager asked me if I would take my pony and run a race with another little boy that had his pony with him, and he offered two dollars for the one that won the race. After some time I decided I would try, and I was glad afterwards because I won the race.

It was getting dark now and we decided we had better get ready and go home, so we hitched up "Captain" and rode around the picnic grounds a while and finally started on our journey homeward. We arrived home safely late that evening and were all very tired after our splendid time at the picnic.

I have taken "Captain" into nearly every store and house in town. He is so gentle and tame and seems to understand everything we say to him. I can never thank the Webb Publishing Company enough for sending "Captain" way out here to me.

I will now tell you about my pony "Marmalade" that came all the way from St. Paul, Minn., to Sunny California.

One day I happened to find a paper with ever so many ponies in it, and as I always wanted one I became very much interested in it and wanted to try and win one of those dear ponies that the Webb Publishing Co. were giving away to girls and boys.

So I sent in my name and got started in the contest. At first it seemed hard as I never had tried anything like that, but The Farmer's Wife is such a nice paper that I had no trouble at all in getting subscribers so I kept right on until the finish, and you don't know how glad I was when I received word that I had won a pony by the name of "Marmalade," and he was to be shipped to me.

One evening when the telephone rang and the agent at the station said the pony had come, I just couldn't wait until papa would bring him home, so I begged real hard to go along, although it was past my bed time.

At last we got started on our way and when we returned home it was ten o'clock. "Marmalade" arrived late at night and I knew that he was very hungry so we gave him a good

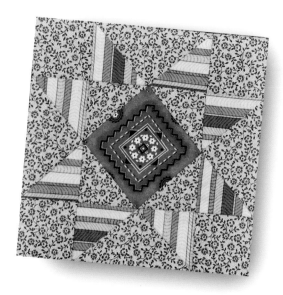

Crystal Star (cy)

Perfectly at Home

60

supper and a drink of water and then made him a nice bed.

So I said good-night to my new friend and went to bed to dream of the lovely times we now would have. He is the sweetest little pet you could ever want, and I am sure he loves his new home.

Whenever he sees me he neighs and comes running and I know that he is begging for an apple or some cake. We have a little calf on the ranch and "Marmalade" and "Jim" are the best of chums. They play all day long in the tall grass and in the evening they come back to the barn.

I have taught him a few tricks such as shaking his head for no and yes, and he can now walk down and up the steps as well as anyone. I can't tell you all the good times my playmates and I have with "Marmalade," and I thank the Webb Publishing Co. many times for giving him to me.

A Happy Pair Posing for Their Picture

61

I wish I could tell every little boy and girl about our pony "Sunshine" and how happy my brother and I were the day he came. When we started out to get subscribers to win a pony, people would tell us we were foolish and the Webb Publishing Company never gave away real live ponies, and then I would go home and cry, for my brother and I both wanted a pony so bad. But we kept right on trying our very best.

Then the contest finally closed and all we could think of or talk about was our pony, wondering if we would sure win one. Several days had passed by and we had not heard a word and we all began to think there was nothing to it. Then Sunday morning came and we were all going in the country to spend the day. So after we got in the auto to go we children asked Papa if he would drive down past the post office to see if we had heard anything. So we did, and sure enough there was a letter from the Webb Publishing Co. and Papa came back out to the car and handed it to me. Oh my! I was so nervous I could not open it, so Mama had to open it and read it to us and it read something like this, "We know you will be glad

Dakota Star (da)

Riding Tandem

62

to hear you have won "Sunshine" and his outfit, which will be shipped you at once." Oh! Dear, can you imagine how we acted? We just laughed and cried both. Then Darold and I just would not go in the country until we went down to the church where my grandma and grandpa were and called them out of the church and told them about it, and they were just about as excited as we were. By Monday morning everybody in Wessington knew that we had won "Sunshine."

Then several days passed by and our pony had not yet come and nearly everybody was saying we would not get a pony, and I just about made up my mind the same way till one morning when the 10:30 train came in, there was "Sunshine." They brought him down to the house in the dray. Our house is just across the street from the schoolhouse and we were at school, but we did not stay there long after we saw the pony. Neither did the rest of the children. Our yard was full in five minutes after "Sunshine" was uncrated. There was no more school for the rest of that day. We were so happy we did not know what to do. We could hardly stay away from him long enough to eat our meals.

continued on next page

MY DARLING PONY "RAY"
IRENE A. BROOKS, CHESHIRE CO., NEW HAMPSHIRE

I am not going to drive "Ray" any this summer or ride him, just let him enjoy life. He is just too cute for anything. I am going to teach him to say his prayers and then I am going to take him to Sunday School with me. Everyone is just wild over him.

Thank you again for your kindness for I do think you are the best club in the world.

continued

It was several more days before the buggy came. We were so well pleased with the buggy and so was "Sunshine." He would just trot along so proud, just as though he knew he was won in a contest.

I wish I could tell you of all the good times we have had with "Sunshine," but it would take a whole magazine to do it, but I am going to tell you one of the best times we have had. My brother and another little boy, seven years old and I drove to my Uncle's who lives eight miles from town. This was quite a ways so we started early in the morning before it got so warm. We did not know much about ponies so did not know just what they could stand. So I made the boys get out and walk up every hill and we stopped at two or three houses on the way down and back too, and watered him. We stopped at the alfalfa fields and picked alfalfa and fed him several times. While he ate alfalfa we picked flowers and decorated his harness all up till he just looked too cute for anything. Now, I am not going to tell you how long it took us to go down or come back, for we took our time at it and mama and papa have laughed at us so much about it, but "Sunshine" had just as much fun out of it as we did.

Now, I will tell you what "Sunshine" likes to eat. He will eat any kind of fruit. We will put a big dish of fruit on the table out on the screened porch, such as apples, grapes, peaches

Sunshine (su)

and plums and you just ought to see him eat them. He is just crazy about them. He does lots of cute tricks but I just can't tell you all of them, but I want to say we would not take $500.00 for him.

Now, I want to tell you a little about ourselves and the Webb Publishing Company, then I will quit. I am a little girl ten years old. I

64

have just one brother seven years old. We both worked together very hard for "Sunshine," so you see "Sunshine" is just as much Darold's as he is mine.

I want to tell all the boys and girls that I feel well paid for all the work that I did in the con-

test and the Webb Publishing Company will do for you just what they say and they certainly give away nice ponies. Don't be afraid to try in their contests.

Three of a Kind—All Happy

*D*art has come! You cannot imagine what that short sentence means to my sister and I, who have always dreamed of owning a Shetland and now to have it come true!

"Dart" is a dear little fellow, as gentle as a kitten, following us wherever we go. When we go to see the neighbors, which is nearly every afternoon, we just take the harness off and turn him loose. When we are ready to go, we will find him near by waiting for us. He has learned several cute tricks, one of which is to lie down and roll and then play sick. We put pillows under his head and cover him up and it takes a good lump of sugar to cure him.

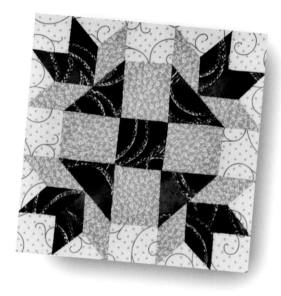

Doe and Darts (dd)

When we first received "Dart," we went for a short ride and in turning a bend of the creek an automobile came suddenly down upon us. We were frightened nearly to death, but the man stopped the car and "Dart" walked up and smelled of it. After that we knew he was perfectly safe.

Our pony had long shaggy hair when he came but now he has shed that off and is as slick and shiny as any horse.

I would like to tell all the boys and girls who want a pony that if they work faithfully in one of your contests, they are sure to win, for we know the Webb Publishing

Fern and "Dart" in the Mountains

Company is strictly on the square and do just what they say they will. There is no need to be discouraged because one lives in a small place, for where we live there are only two families, the one who has the store and the family at the hotel. People who took the paper to help us get the pony and outfit have since told us what a fine one it is and that they like it very much better than other papers they are taking. Others who tried to discourage us by saying it would just be some "cheap John" outfit have since had to acknowledge that everything is strictly first-class and as good as money could buy.

The night "Dart" came one of the neighbor boys, a little fellow four years old, came running over and said, "Girls, I am almost as tickled as you are."

I wish to thank you again for "Dart" and the outfit, and hope many other little boys and girls can get one as good.

"It Takes a Good Lump of Sugar to Cure Him"

67

How We Won "Cinders"

We joined The Farmer's Wife Pony Club with the idea of winning if it was in us to do so. The paper sold very well but we found quite a few people that wanted to take it that did not have the money, so we took their order and told them we would call for the money later. Of course, that was extra work but we did not mind, for we finally won "Cinders" and he is just a dandy. He is sorrel and white and the prettiest one we have ever seen.

Papa made a portable yard for "Cinders" that is sixteen feet square and put together with hinges so it will fold up when not in use. I put him in out in the field and we move it around from place to place so he has nice green grass all the time and we know right where he is.

One morning we were a little late in starting for school and papa did not say anything to us but went out to the barn and harnessed up our pony to a little buggy that he had just made over and when we came out we were surprised to see "Cinders" all ready at the door. Papa said, "Come on and I will take you to school." Ralph and I got in and the pony was off like a shot for school. When we got down on to Main St. the children were just going to school and it was funny to see about fifty children running along behind us, but "Cinders" did not mind it a bit, if anything it made him go faster. When we reached the school house we were surrounded by all the boys and girls in the school, teachers and all, and they all wanted to pat the pony. He

Elsie's Favorite (ef)

shook hands with everyone that could reach him and they were just crazy about him.

I know you would laugh if you could see my brother playing cowboy. He fastens a rope around the cow's horns and plays he has roped a steer.

My papa works nights and when he comes home about 12 o'clock he goes out to see "Cinders" and he seems to be waiting for him. He always brings him home something to eat, candy or something sweet. Papa has taught "Cinders" to follow him around. Sometimes he will start down the street on the run and the pony after him. Just as he gets almost up to him, papa turns around and runs the other way and it is so cute to see "Cinders" turn after him.

We live near quite a large town where they have street cars and one day I was riding "Cinders" along the street when one of the street car conductors said, "Don't you want a ride?" and I said "Yes, if you will take the pony, too."

He said, "Come on," and I led the pony over to the car and he was going right in but we thought that would hardly do for the conductor might lose his job. He did not think I could get the pony on, but I guess he don't know how much you can do with a pony if you are kind to him and have a little patience.

We just love to live a long way from school. Now, we sometimes wish it was farther because "Cinders" takes us along so nice and is not afraid of anything. He don't mind an auto any more than he does a wheel-barrow.

Don't let anyone persuade you that you can't get one, for you are sure to if you only try. We feel so pleased with ours that we want every boy and girl to have one and be as happy as we are.

"Papa Made a Little Portable Yard"

One evening last winter my papa was reading in his farm paper where the Webb Publishing Company gave ponies away to boys and girls who worked for them. Papa wrote them that night and as soon as I heard from them I joined the Pony Club and started to work selling papers.

I wrote to my Aunt in Tennessee and Uncle in Kentucky asking them to help me secure subscribers, which they did willingly. My grandma, who is sick and seldom leaves her home, sold many papers for me by asking everyone who came to her house. Of course, they all took the paper from her because they knew what joy it would be to her to see me win a darling pony of my own. It seemed to be no trouble for everyone that helped me as well as myself, to sell the paper because it was such a good everyday paper.

Some times I would have people say discouraging things to me about the Webb Publishing Company not treating me fair, but I just kept on working all the more because I wanted to show them the faith I had in the Webb Publishing Company.

When the letter came telling me I had won "Rustler," mamma did not tell me because she wanted to surprise me. I did not know it until the night of his arrival, which was the night before Easter Sunday. My papa sent our driver to the depot to see if "Rustler" was there and sure enough he was, the dearest Easter gift in the world. He took him out of his crate and led him

Eastertide Quilt (eq)

home. I was sitting in the dining room when I noticed mamma jump up and run to the door at the sound of something walking through the store. He was brought through the store into the dining room and right away brother and I saddled him and rode him around the room. We hugged and kissed him many times that night. He seemed to know that he was at home and there was a nice box stall and a good supper awaiting him.

Nobody can imagine how surprised and overjoyed I was to know that I had won "Rustler." I was the happiest girl in the world that night and I think it was the longest night I ever spent in my life for I could hardly wait to see him in the daylight.

The next day was Easter Sunday. Papa turned him loose in the yard to eat grass and roll. There were many visitors to see him that day and for many days afterwards. His coat was very shaggy when he first came, but as soon as the weather was warm enough, we had him clipped and he soon became a beautiful pony.

continued on next page

They All Say, "Look at the Sweet Little Pony"

"POP"

DOUGLAS LOCKMAN, CROCKETT CO., TENNESSEE

I have not got to ride much on account of my arm which I broke sometime ago but I enjoy seeing my little sister ride him. We had a big road rally here on the 16th and I wish you could have seen sister and "Pop" in the parade.

I am ten years old and have been paralyzed ever since I was five and I cannot play games with the other boys and I have always wanted a pony.

continued

Every morning "Rustler" is well groomed and is fed a good breakfast with an egg put in his feed and an apple for dessert.

I tied him in front of our store every day before my buggy came and several times people would come up and ask where I bought him. One day a stranger came over where "Rustler" was tied and asked if I would sell him, but of course I said, "No, I will not sell him for any price."

Several weeks after my pony came, I was riding him one day when a little neighbor boy wanted to ride. The saddle turned with him and he fell off. Away went "Rustler" trotting down the road and over to the depot where a crowd of people was standing. He stopped by them as if to say, "Somebody catch me." When we caught him a man with two children came over and asked me if I would sell him. When I said no, he asked me where I got him. You bet I was so proud of such a proud little runaway that I was delighted to tell him all particulars.

"Rustler" is not afraid of autos, but is always full of life and attracts the attention of many people who say, "Look at the sweet little pony." I have not yet taught him many tricks but intend doing so.

I have lived behind a grocery store in town all my life. Brother and I have never been very strong, being afflicted with throat trouble. Our doctor told papa to move to the country,

Rambling Road (rr)

so he decided to take us all and "Rustler" and move to the country for the summer. When we go in town my friends tell me that it is hard to tell which has helped me the most, the country or "Rustler," because I have grown so much stronger through living out of doors with "Rustler."

Since I have had the joy of owning a pony I would love to see every boy and girl win one and would be glad to write any boy or girl who writes me for information.

Some day I would take great pleasure in meeting the Pony Editor who makes it possible for girls to win ponies of their own. I would thank him a thousand times for helping me.

OFF FOR OUR MORNING EXERCISE
IMOGENE SCHWARTZ, MONTGOMERY CO., MARYLAND

LITTLE FRIEND "FLIP"

When "Flip" came I was at school. He came about ten o'clock. When I came home he was out in the lawn eating grass. I went up to him and put my arms

around his neck and Oh! how I did hug him. I was so glad that I had won him. He was so tired and sleepy from being on the train so long but I gave him a good supper and made him a nice little straw bed.

73

Some time ago we received letters from the Webb Publishing Company telling us of the splendid opportunity of gaining one of their ponies. For a long time it had been my dream unrealized but now the time was at hand, and the next day the mailman carried the letter to the post office.

I am eight years old and my sister Ella, who is eleven years old, helped me get subscribers.

We were discouraged on hearing that we had not won one of the ponies in the contest. But that was soon over; the Webb Publishing Company, being so kind and generous, gave us an extra chance and then we got "Reno." "Reno" was a favorite name so we named him that although his first name was "Merry."

Late in the evening of July 15th, we received a message telling us of his arrival. It was a stormy evening and they had taken him to the livery barn, and during that time until he arrived a number of children had begun to make friends with him. We started for town at 7 o'clock the next morning and as we live six miles away, the way seemed twice as long. When we got there we heard some other boys and girls cry because "Reno" was going to

Ella's Star (es)

"My Turn Next"

leave, and some said, "How much will you take for him." Others, "Can't I buy him?" Surely he is the cutest animal and best chum known.

He is only about two years old so we do not ride him much, although we got a beautiful saddle and bridle free. Whenever we call his name he comes running to us, always looking for some bread and butter, a few plums or an apple. He just loves milk and crackers. Often he comes up on our back porch and one day my big sister had a piece of cake in her hand which he wanted. She jumped into the woodshed for fun and closed the door, but "Reno" was not baffled by that. He cocked his little ears and walked smartly up to the door knob and opened it with his teeth, and received an apple as a reward. "Shepherd," our dog, and "Reno" are great friends. Sometimes he takes long strolls around the farm, eating grass accompanied by "Shepherd." What I think he is fondest of is a sugar lump and ground oats.

I think "Reno" must be a little lonesome when we are at school because he is so glad when we

"The Cutest and Best Chum"

get back. He rubs his nose against our sleeves and follows us wherever we go. It is good for little girls to own a pony, keeping them interested and in the fresh air.

He always uses his front feet in kicking over pails and buckets after drinking milk. "Reno" knows how to take our hats off and also spit out the stones when eating plums.

I would not part with "Reno" for anything for I love him too well and would miss him just awful. We curry his mane every day so that it will grow thick and long and he likes it, too.

One day while we had the threshers, we took him along to the machine to see if he was scared, but of course he wasn't. He only stared a little and looked up to us in the grain box and whinnied to us as if to say "Take good care of me." He is not at all afraid of autos or motorcycles.

Enough praise cannot be given to the Webb Publishing Company for giving out such dear little ponies, making so many little children happy, and I am sure that they will reap their reward some day.

75

I am a little boy ten years old, four feet and eleven inches tall. I weigh 87 pounds and have light hair and blue eyes. But what I want to tell you about is my pony "Sonny" which the Webb Publishing Company gave me. "Sonny" is the finest pony in these parts and he and his outfit are better than five hundred dollars to me.

I went to the depot to meet my pony the day he came. I could hear him whinnying but I could not see him. Then I went to the other side of the car and I saw him in a little crate on the express wagon ready to go to the express office. I took him out of the crate and the people laughed at me and told me he was a little sheep lamb, he was so woolly looking in his winter coat. Papa told me to give him some water but he couldn't reach the fountain that big horses used. I told them that was all right and I told them if they were such a little pony as that they couldn't reach the fountain either. And then I brought him home and my uncle told me he was a dear little plaything. The next time I went to town he looked so well they all wanted to buy him. I told them no money would buy him. He is the smallest and cutest pony around here. He gained 45 pounds the first four months after I got him.

One day I drove "Sonny" to a picnic and my brother went with me and when we got there a lot of people came around and admired him. We unhitched him and tied him up and then some boys and girls crawled through in under him and the boys gave him some water and picked grass

Flying Clouds (fc)

for the pony. Some of the boys and girls said to me that they had more picnic with the pony then with anything else. Then a big black cloud came up and the people got excited and thought they had better start home. Papa told me I had better start too or I would get my buggy muddy, but "Sonny" kept up with the other teams all the way back to the farm.

"Sonny" goes as fast as he can when we go after the cows nights. We are such good little friends and he never runs away or kicks me. He is always around the house or barn. "Sonny" is always around when meal time comes. Sometimes when I am riding him he turns around short and I fall off and "Sonny" stands and looks at me and laughs because it is a good joke. "Sonny" and I run races horseback with the other boys. Almost every time he and I beat.

As I don't always like to use my nice buggy I made a little roller cart and I can have lots of fun with it. First I took an old vinegar barrel and nailed some cleats on both ends, then to these I fastened a block with a bolt which takes the place of an axle. The shafts and seat fit over this bolt, and are held in place by a nut. I also had to fasten the seat to the shafts so that it would not fall over backwards. Then I made some places on the shafts to put my feet on just like the real jockeys have on their racing rigs. When it was all finished I had a fine roller cart as you can see by the picture. Quite often I invite my little boy and girl friends from the farms near my home to come and play with "Sonny" and me, and we have the best times. We all take turns riding on the cart and my little friends enjoy it as much as I do.

I am never going to sell "Sonny" and he is so good that he makes me feel happy all the time.

"Sonny" Holding a Reception for All His Little Friends

One day not long ago my mother was reading a farm journal, and she saw a picture of "Cub" hitched up all ready for a drive. She called me to her and said, "Son, now here's a chance to win a pony." I had been wanting just such a pony for a long time because I live two miles outside of town and I have often thought how much fun it would be to have a little pony and ride to town and school.

I was a little afraid to start in the contest because the time was so near up for it was then about the middle of November and the contest was to close December 16th. I thought about nothing else but that dear little pony for the next day or two, wishing I could get it, and decided I would make a try for it anyhow. Mamma and daddy finally agreed to let me try for it and told me I would have to hustle good and proper if I got enough subscribers to get it. I went to work right then, and got several subscribers nearly every day until the very last.

My but it was a long time having to wait to hear about who got it. I told mamma and daddy that I didn't want Santa to bring me a thing, all I wanted was "Cub" and the outfit. I thought I ought to hear something

Good Cheer (gc)

"'Cub' Likes to Carry Double"

Christmas Eve anyway but Christmas Eve came and not a word. I was awfully disappointed for it seemed then I had failed, and dear old Santa felt so sorry for me he went up town and got me a gold watch. So I just gave it up and expected nothing but some nice prize for my work.

Somehow or other I kept on hoping, and called up the express man the morning after Christmas and he said "Cub" was there. My! but I danced and hollered and cut up all sorts of capers till the folks thought I had just about gone crazy, I was so happy! I have two sisters smaller than I am, and they were most as happy as I was. I ran right out and got on the car and went to town and got "Cub" right out of the express office and rode him home. He is the prettiest and dearest little pony I ever saw and the harness and little buggy are just fine! In the winter his hair is long and shaggy and he looks just like a big fuzzy dog. You can see in the pictures how long his hair was last Winter. In the summer though, his hair sheds off and he shines like satin. I can't tell you how much I thank the Webb Publishing Co., but just a whole lot, of course, and will always remember them as long as I live.

"Looks Like a Big Fuzzy Dog"

THE RIGHT "SPOT"

I had always wanted a pony but I never dreamed of earning one myself until one day I saw an advertisement in a paper, saying I could earn one like so many other little boys and girls had done. After getting mamma's and papa's consent to write and see what work I had to do, I wrote. In a few days a letter came from the Webb Publishing Company, telling what I should do and I started at once to work. People did not seem to think very much of getting a pony in this way and many prophesied that there would be no pony given at all, but I worked on until the last minute.

One day when papa was in town, he got a letter saying I had won "Spot." Papa knew how anxious I was, so he telephoned to me. Even after this letter came many said it was all a fake and that I would not get it.

One day grandpa, who had come home on the same train with "Spot," telephoned that my pony had come and that he would help take him from the car. A great many people watched us lead him home. Everyone wanted to see "Spot" as soon as they heard I had won him. All those who saw him thought him very pretty.

"Spot" soon learned to do some very cute tricks. One day while I was petting him he got a hold of my hair ribbon and pulled it off. Before I could get it away from him, he had it all chewed up. Another time while I was at Mr. King's on "Spot" Mrs. King came in from the garden with a head of cabbage in her hand. She came up to

Girl's Favorite (gf)

pet "Spot." He did not wait to be asked to have some cabbage, but reached out his head and began to help himself.

We always carry feed in a tin tub to the barn. When "Spot" hears the rattle of the tub he comes running to get something to eat. One day mamma got some kindling in the tub instead of feed and "Spot" followed her nearly all the way to the house, thinking that the kindling was feed.

I would not take any amount of money for "Spot" and the dear little saddle and bridle that the Webb Publishing Company sent me for so little work.

I wish to thank the Webb Publishing Company for the pony and I will tell all the little boys and girls who want one, how they can earn one as I did.

"'Spot' Soon Learned to Do Cute Tricks"

MY PONY "LEE"
MABEL MYERS, MINNEHAHA CO., SOUTH DAKOTA

"Lee" is useful to us all. Three times a week I go to town with him and get the ice. I have a little wagon I tie behind the buggy to carry the ice in, and I also get the groceries for mamma and my brother and I go after the cows every night.

"Lee" is a sweet playful and useful little fellow and I feel so thankful to know I am his mistress.

I want to write and tell you something about my dear little "Honey," she is so cunning.

I received my wagon and harness Saturday night, October 17th. I could hardly wait to see it put together. It certainly is just lovely. I cannot tell you how proud I am of my prize. We worked real hard to get it, but I think I could afford to work again just as hard to get an outfit, if I did not have one of my own. Almost every one that sees it thinks it just grand.

"Honey" is a little thin now but she will soon get fat. I think her long trip was enough to make a big horse thin, riding so far. She rode three days and two nights. Poor little thing, she was so tired and hungry.

She loved me from the very first I know for she will let me do anything with her. Sometimes when I get home from school when I go to lead her to water or give her some clover, she will shake her head no, but I will whisper to her, "Come 'Honey' and I will give you something nice, a russet apple, or some oats, sugar or something like that;" then she walks along with me just as nice. She will shake hands with me. Sometimes I will say, "Hello, 'Honey'" and she will answer me. I have ridden her several times and drove her first, so

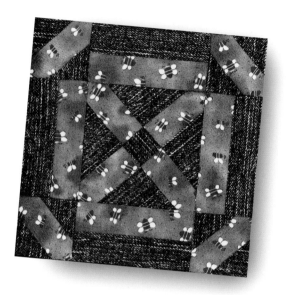

Girl's Joy (gj)

My Little Dog Rides "Honey"

have not had time to teach her many tricks as I go to school every day. She knows we love her dearly. She will put her little head on my shoulder and I will hug and kiss her. She loves to have me hug her. Sometimes I take my book down to the barn and sit in "Honey's" box stall and read. She will come and stand right beside me.

As I have no brothers or sisters to play with I think I have one of just the nicest little playmates that ever was. We run and play together and we think so much of each other. Papa and mama love her too. I don't know how I could get along without her now.

There have been so many little girls and boys who wrote to me and asked if I really did get a pony and outfit, or if it was all a bluff. I wrote and told them that I really did get a live pony and my prize was well worth working for too. Some would say to me when I was canvassing, "Did you ever know of any one that got a pony?" We told them we knew of one and had heard of one little boy that lived in Fulton. They did not want to believe us so when my little pony gets a little older, I want to drive to some of these places and just show them my pony.

"Honey" is not afraid of automobiles or threshing machines, so another year I think I can drive her a great deal.

"Honey" Arriving in Her Little Crate

I have the dearest little brown and white Shetland pony which the Webb Publishing Company sent me free all the way from St. Paul, Minn., away out here to Ionia Co., Mich. He is the cutest little pony I ever saw and everyone says so that sees him. He is just as kind and gentle as he can be and is just as handsome as you find them. He just makes his little feet and legs fly when going down the road hitched to his little buggy and surely does make the dust fly. He is also a fine saddler. I have enjoyed many a ride this summer and as my health is poor he is just the nicest kind of out door playmate and I enjoy his company very much. I can harness and hitch him up alone. I take my little friends all for a ride.

And now I'll tell you how I won "Snap."

I wrote to the Webb Publishing Company to see what I would have to do to win a pony. They wrote back to me and told me they wished me to get subscribers for The Farmer's Wife. I commenced work close at home with my dog "Trim" for which I have a harness and wagon (he has drawn one around for several years). I did so well getting subscriptions that my grandparents began helping me; although they were very busy they would hitch up and drive a long distance

Grandmother's Favorite (gm)

"Snap" and His New Friends

BY JENNIE NADEAU, IONIA CO., MICHIGAN

with me and so we worked until at last the time expired and then I was anxious to know whether I had won a pony or not.

One day I received a letter saying I had won "Snap" and it made me very happy. Then I received a letter telling me they had sent "Snap" by express and would be here on a certain day. I could hardly wait but one evening we got a telephone call from Belding saying my pony had come. I was so delighted I jumped right up and down and all I could say was, "My pony has come, my pony has come."

We went right over to Belding in an automobile and brought Mr. Pony back in the automobile from there. When "Snap" arrived he was a little hungry and tired but was alright next day, so I put his saddle and bridle on him and enjoyed a ride.

No amount of money could buy "Snap." I feed him, curry him and give him his baths, (he loves to have a bath).

I know I could not get along without him now. He is so much company for me as I live with my grandpa and grandma and there are no children for me to play with. Two of my sisters and a cousin were here to visit me this summer and we had many good times with "Snap." My grandpa made a stone boat for me and I drew up corn and potatoes and cabbage with him. He is a stout little fellow and feels very proud when he is working. I intended driving "Snap" in the parade at the Labor Day picnic this fall but had to give it up on account of my sickness. I hope the outdoor exercise with "Snap" will improve my health and make me stronger.

continued on page 87

"Off for a Spin Down the Road, 'Snap' Just Makes His Little Feet Fly"

85

I thought I would write you a few lines to let you know how "Pat" is doing. "Pat" and I are getting along just fine. He is gaining and is as fat as a little pig. I have got him on good grass and I feed him three times a day an ear of corn and a pint of oats, and every morning and evening he has to have a drink of fresh milk beside what other little stuff I feed him, in fact most every thing but meat. He will not eat meat. I don't see what makes him pick up so. He does not eat so awfully much. Of course he eats a little but not very much.

I try to get time to take a pleasure ride every day and I think more of him every time that I ride him for he is such a nice saddler. He lopes right along and carries you just as easy as if you were rocking in a cradle. We have an orchard of about two acres and when I let him out of the lawn into the orchard he just rolls and kicks and runs for about an hour, just as fast as he can jump, and every one that sees him says that he is the cutest little pony they ever saw. I wouldn't take a thousand dollars for him today.

"Pat" is round as an apple, as slick as a mole and ready to go whenever he is told. He just enjoys going after the cows

Gold Nuggets (gn)

"He Is Such a Nice Saddler"

86

and sheep of evenings. I carry a lunch twice a day to the field for my father and brother and he likes to go to the field for they always invite "Pat" to eat with them and he always accepts the invitation. He is very fond of bread, butter, pie and cake and jells of all sorts. He weighed 255 pounds when I got him and his weight at the present time is 355 pounds.

I ride "Pat" to town about twice a week and the children gather around with something for him to eat. The people say he is the finest pony that ever came to town. The people say they think The Farmer's Wife paper is just the one and some say that they could not get along without it and I know I could not get along without "Pat." He is thoroughly broke and will do anything you tell him to do if he can but he can't talk Dutch.

I feel so thankful that I ever joined the Pony Club and many thanks to you and your kindness in the way you have been to me and for "Pat." He is worth his weight in gold. Give my love to all members.

WHAT "SNAP" MEANS TO ME
continued from page 85

"Snap" loves oats, corn, apples and he also likes candy and sugar. He often comes to the door—comes right up on the back porch and looks through the screen door, teasing for something good to eat and I never refuse giving him something.

I love my dear little pony "Snap" and "Snap" loves me better than anyone else and I am very grateful to the Webb Publishing Company for sending me such a beautiful playmate and hope they will make lots of other children as happy.

I want to tell every boy and girl that loves animals, especially a pony, as well as I do how they can get one and how I got mine. The contest had been going on about a month when one day my sister Mildred came running to me crying, "Oh Getty, Getty, look here, a pony free to any boy or girl who is willing to work for him." She read the papers all through to me telling about what we should do. We decided immediately to go to work, but my mamma said, "Oh Gretchen, what is the use, you can never win one of those ponies." I said, "I know I can and I am going to try if you will let me." And I cried so hard that mamma said, "Well, you may try but I don't think it will do you any good." I went to work with a will.

My sister and I were out one whole day and we didn't get one subscription and we were so disappointed we were almost afraid to go the next day. But finally I did, and I began to have better luck and in a short time I was getting so many names, papa and even mamma began to get interested. So much so that they helped get subscribers for me. One day an old gentleman, a great friend of mine, said, "I will go with you around the town (as you know I am just a little girl seven years old) if you will do all the talking." I agreed to do that and that day I got quite a few subscriptions for The Farmer's Wife.

Some people I went to tried to discourage me and would not take my paper. Others said, "I would take the paper but it won't do you any

Gretchen (gr)

good." But I kept right on and if you should try to win a pony, don't let such things discourage you, but work with might and main and I am sure you will win. You will win something any way because the Webb Publishing Company is honorable in all their transactions and did by me just as they said they would.

When the contest was over you don't know how anxiously I waited to hear, and when I found out I was to get a dear little pony my happiness knew no bounds. They brought him

by Gretchen M. Stelzer, Summit Co., Ohio

Isn't He Pretty?

up from the depot one forenoon while I was at school, and when I came home and they told me he was out in the barn, I could hardly wait to get out there. I went into his box stall papa had made for him and he and I were friends at once. At first he would try to nip me. Now he just licks my hands and face and takes my hair ribbons off. He will shake hands with me and put both his front feet in my hands standing straight up on his hind feet. The other day he followed me up on the front porch out through the living room, dining room and kitchen. I gave him a slice of bread. He ate it and then followed me out into the yard again.

continued on next page

Doesn't Seem Possible
Lloyd Thomas, Allen Co., Ohio

I am crippled and it was hard for me to get around. My mamma saw the Webb Publishing Company advertising a pony outfit and thought it would be nice for me. I did not think it was any use for me to try, but she urged me and so I won a beautiful pony which I call "Flo." Everybody says she is the nicest pony they ever saw. I have more fun with her than anything I ever had. I have had so many people who wanted to buy her, but I would not take anything for her.

continued

His name is "Welkie" and whenever I call him
he will answer me. I think everything of him and
no money could buy him from me. I love him so
and mamma says The Farmer's Wife is one of the
best little papers she has ever read and the recipes
that she has tried in it are excellent and different
ones that took the paper from me here, told me
since that they like it as well as any magazine they
ever had.

Although I have written a long story already
I am going to say a little more because there are
some more of his tricks to tell you about and some
more good things, also, about The Farmer's Wife.

I must tell you about what one lady who had
subscribed for The Farmer's Wife when I was
in the contest said to me the other day. I was
going along the street thinking about some more
people who might want to take the magazine and
I heard some one call, "Hello, Gretchen, come
here." I looked around and saw
a lady standing in her door and I
went up to her. She said, "You can
just tell everybody that I feel repaid
ten times over for the price of The
Farmer's Wife by finding one lace
pattern in it. I had for several years
wanted a pattern for 'Clover Leaf
Lace' but was not successful in
finding it until I found it in the June
issue of The Farmer's Wife. In fact,
I find that each and every issue has

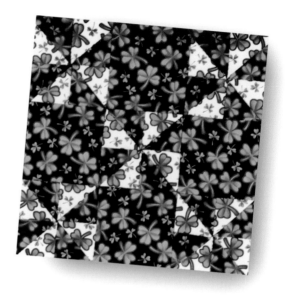

Clover Leaf (cv)

"Welkie" Is Small but He Can Keep Up

90

in it some recipe, pattern, household hint or story that, of itself, is easily worth the whole price of the paper." You may be sure that I was much pleased to have such a good recommendation of the magazine that helped me to get my pony.

"Welkie" is growing larger and getting more cunning every day. One day my auntie went out to see him and she had some crocheted buttons on her dress and he tried to eat them right off of her dress. Whenever I go out to him and have anything to eat in my hand he wants me to give him some of it and I always do. Sometimes I pretend I do not see him and I will try to pass by him without noticing him but he will stretch his neck and put up his foot to stop me as much as to say, "I'm here. Don't you see me?" Of course then I stop and pet him as I meant to all the time anyway.

Now all you boys and girls who want a pony, get busy. See your friends and try hard and you will surely get one, for the Webb Publishing Company will do all that it promises to do.

"TOBY" LOOKS ROUGH IN HIS WINTER HAIR
GEORGE I. LYNCH, LAKE CO., ILLINOIS

"Toby" is certainly the dearest pony of the bunch. I never knew what it was to be happy before I got "Toby." He dearly loves me and I do him. He stands on a box, rolls a barrel and puts his front feet on papa's shoulder and then bounds to the ground. My little brother, four years old, rides him all over and he will follow me into the house if he thinks I have sugar, cake or apples. He doesn't look very nice in the picture but he is very pretty when his hair sheds off.

I will write and tell you how glad I was when I won "Chick." The first day I went to town to meet "Chick" he wasn't there, also the second time, but the third day my uncle went to town and "Chick" was waiting at the depot for someone to take him and great crowds of children and grown-up people were standing around him. Then "Chick" had to ride fifteen miles yet. When he came it was dark already and uncle called us to come out doors. My! how glad we all were, for we knew "Chick" had come. He looked so tired but his eyes were very bright. He looked as if he was glad he had come to his new home at last.

We took him out of the crate and put him in the barn. He was all tired out from his long journey. I could not sleep that night and wait till morning would come, so got up early the next morning and of course the first thing I did was to go and see my dear little pony. As soon as the neighbors heard that "Chick" had arrived, they were so surprised that the first thing they could do was to come and see him. Some said, "Although we bought a subscription from you we never thought you would get a pony." For about two weeks people were continually coming and going, all complimenting and praising "Chick."

We have lots of fun with "Chick." We make parades and play circus in which "Chick" is always the actor. He knows all sorts of tricks and games. He can play hide-and-go-seek, shake hands, stand with his front feet on a chair and comes running when you call him, for he surely

Hen and Her Chicks (hc)

expects something good to eat. He eats bread, sugar, vegetables, candy and especially apples.

One day he climbed up the steps and got on the porch, pushed the screen door and came in but the door into the kitchen was shut so he rapped on the door with his foot. He wanted to come in and we all watched him to see what he would do. Finally he turned the knob and came in. We all had to laugh at him being so smart and now he comes in the house every day for something to eat.

My sister and I ride "Chick" to school and when we get there we make him go home and in the evening mother sends him to school after us. The neighbors are surprised to see him trot to school to get us home. When he comes to school he stands by the door and waits for us. He made this trip three times already and so we hope he will keep it up. All the children are glad to see him come and they all share their lunch with him.

If any girl or boy wishes to get a pony, I advise them to enter the Pony Club for they surely will be rewarded for little work. I can never thank the Webb Publishing Company enough for sending "Chick" to me.

"'Chick' Entertains Me and All My Friends"

When I first read about the Webb Publishing Co. giving away ponies to boys and girls, I could hardly believe it. I wanted to try and win one because Shetland Ponies are such jolly play-fellows and such dear pets.

I started out to work and won "Bingo." We were all so happy when I received a telegram, Christmas eve, saying that I had won "Bingo," and could hardly wait until Christmas day to see him. He came on the noon train and from the very first he behaved perfectly and he is the dearest and best pony any child could have.

I think almost everyone within ten or fifteen miles came to see "Bingo." They did not seem to believe that the Webb Publishing Company or anyone would give a real live pony away. They all thought he was a splendid pony and how fortunate I was to win him.

When I first got "Bingo," he weighed two hundred eighty pounds, but now he weighs three hundred pounds. When my friends ask me if "Bingo" is afraid of automobiles and such things, I am very glad to say that he is not.

"Bingo" knows several tricks; he can shake hands and stand on a chair or box. I will now tell you how he acts in parades. He was in the Fourth of July parade. "Bingo" seems to know just when to turn the corners and follow the ones in front. There was a large rooster walking in front of him, but he did not mind it at all. There was a pony back of us and every once in a while, she would paw on the ground and try

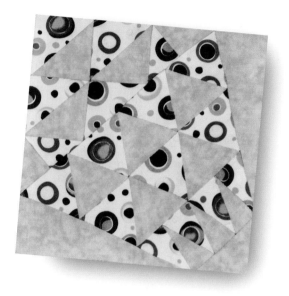

Ice Cream Bowl (ic)

to get down and roll. I was proud to see "Bingo" act so nicely.

"Bingo" does look so funny with his long winter coat of hair, but he is just as dear as ever. When I whistle, or call him he whinners and comes to me.

One day a man said to me, "Will you trade "Bingo" for a forty acre farm?" I told him I would not part with "Bingo" for any amount of money or anything else. Mother and Father love "Bingo" just almost as much as I do. My brother, two sisters and I have been very happy since we received "Bingo." My friends think he is just dear and love him very much. They also enjoy going out riding with him.

I have just earned my first money with "Bingo." The other day I and my brother were out riding when a man came up to us and said: "I can't get anyone to deliver my groceries; could you do it for me if I give you 25 cents?" So I said, "You bet I can." Then we went down to the store and got several boxes of groceries and delivered them. Then the man gave us the money. "Bingo" seemed to enjoy doing it very much and I am glad he did. Maybe I'll make lots of money with him now.

"Bingo" will go in my pockets for apples or anything that is good. He will eat ice cream, peaches, or cherries out of a dish. He likes bread, butter, crackers, cake and cookies. Every time I come into the barn, he will smell around me to see if I have anything and if I have, he will get a hold of it with his teeth and eat it as if it was very good.

"Bingo" has been all over our house except upstairs and we have not taken him up there yet. When I have something good to eat "Bingo" looks up in my face as if to say, "Please give me some for you know I like it so well." Then of course I give it to him right away.

I will say that I love The Farmer's Wife like all the other pony winners for if it were not for their being so loving and kind as to give away a dear little pony like "Bingo" none of the happy children that have ponies would have them.

"Bingo" Ready for the 4th of July Parade

Last Fall I saw a notice in the paper saying that they were going to give away more Shetland ponies with their outfits, and I made up my mind I was going to win one, so I started to work. I thought it was very discouraging as I lived near a very small town and I was afraid that I would not have a chance, but I found that I was mistaken and had as good a chance as any other boy or girl. Some of the people that I asked told me that I was wasting my time and I would not get anything as those kind of offers were all fakes, but I knew that the Webb Publishing Company would surely give me a pony if I got more votes than anyone else, so I kept at it. On Christmas morning when my papa and I went up to the depot there on the platform was a little spotted pony in a crate with lots of people crowding around it and then I knew I had won "Andy," and how happy I was. After we took him out of the crate we led him through town and all the little boys wanted to ride him. We took him into all the stores so that everybody could see him.

For a while after he came there was so much snow on the ground and we could not use the buggy so we hitched him up to a little sled and I used to haul hay to help papa feed the cattle. But now that the snow is off of the ground, I can use my buggy and ride him horseback. I do not ride him to school because the school is right across the road, but the minute school is out, I go and get "Andy" and we play together until dark, for he is the greatest playfellow I or any other boy

Handy Andy (ha)

ever had. I take him in the house and give him sugar and if I am eating an apple he tries to take it away from me. No matter where he is, when he hears me call he comes running up to me and he is as good a chum as another boy would be.

The way I make money with my pony, my papa pays me to drive the cows to and from the pasture, and "Andy" seems to like to chase the cows as well as I do.

Lots of people have wanted to buy my pony but I would not sell him for any money. My papa and mamma are just as proud and happy over my pony as I am, and it keeps me outside in the fresh air all the time, and I have not had a cold since I got my pony. There's no place to live like a ranch, especially if one has a nice Shetland pony for company. I am teaching "Andy" tricks and he will shake hands with me and he will stand on a box to reach sugar and when I am riding him, he will put his front feet up on a box and stand so straight that I nearly slip off.

I think every little boy and girl should have a Shetland pony because it teaches them to handle horses and gives them lots of outdoor exercise and teaches them to be kind and gentle to animals and if they are an only child like I am, it gives them a playfellow and a companion. Taking care of it gives them something useful to do and keeps them out of mischief. I don't know of a nicer way to get one than to get subscribers for the Webb Publishing Company for most of the subscribers that I got say the paper is the best farm paper published. I am glad the Webb Publishing Company gave me a chance to win such a nice pony and outfit without one cent of cost to me and I will always thank them and do what I can for them.

"I am Teaching 'Andy' Tricks"

*O*ne day as I was looking at a paper I saw an advertisement how to win a little Shetland Pony. So I wrote to the Webb Publishing Company and asked them all about it. I soon had a letter from them telling me I had to get subscribers. When I first started out getting subscribers everyone said it was humbug and that I would never win a pony, nothing but a wooden horse. Someone said I would get a stuffed pony and an express wagon while others said I would only get a piece of his tail. But I was so anxious and kept right at it, the more subscribers I got the more interested I got in the contest. When I sent in my last subscriptions I could hardly wait to see if I would be one of the Lucky Pony Winners.

A few days before Xmas I got a telephone call telling me my little pony was at the depot. I did not happen to be at the depot when "Jewel" arrived. But when I reached the depot I found it crowded with children and grown people. They had "Jewel" taken out of the crate and when I rode him to the house a crowd of people followed me like a parade. I certainly felt proud of him. On Xmas eve we went to church and when we came home Santa Claus was here, the Xmas tree was all lit up and we got all our presents. Then I brought "Jewel" in the house too because he was the best present I could wish for. He looked so

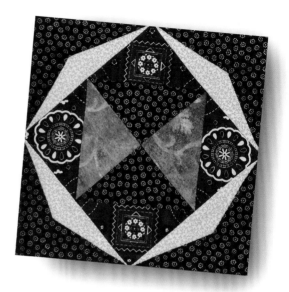

Jewel (je)

"I Would Not Sell My Pony for Any Price"

98

happy. We treated him on candy, apples and cake and he seemed to enjoy his Xmas as well as I did mine. This was the happiest Xmas I had ever had.

I have such good times with "Jewel." I go to picnics, parties and take my little brother and sisters out riding. My friends think just as much of him as I do, in fact everybody in town thinks he is just as dear as he can be. He is not scared of anything: he will hold his nose right up to an automobile if you wish him to and mamma is not afraid to let us go any place with him for she knows we are perfectly safe with "Jewel." I tell you "Jewel" can go some for one day papa and I took a trip in the country about four miles and on the way coming home papa said let's run a race. Papa has a fine bay team, six and seven years old,

so we started out. Papa made his team go as fast as they could and "Jewel" was right behind them. When we got about two blocks from town I gave "Jewel" a tap with the rein and we passed him and beat him home. Papa said he could not see his legs move he went so fast.

"Jewel" likes apples, candy, cake, cookies and in fact anything children like, especially sweet things. He also can do tricks; shake hands, put his front feet on chairs and shake his head for yes or no.

I would not sell my pony for any price. I wish every boy or girl could win such a fine pony and outfit as mine which the Webb Publishing Company gave me and for which I thank them many times.

"We Are Perfectly Safe With 'Jewel'"

I am going to write to you and the Pony Club how I came to work for "Sweetheart." When I was nearly five years old mamma saw in a paper she was taking your advertisement of a pony to be given away for a little work. Mamma told me that if I went in the contest it would mean plenty of work but I wanted to try so we started out. After getting most of our neighbors in the country to subscribe we went into town. Mamma would go with me and stand where she could watch me and I would go up one side of main street and down the other. Sometimes people would say, "Little Dear, I don't think I care for your paper." Then I would thank them and show them my pony pin and often they would call me back and give me a subscription, for I always thanked them the same as though they did subscribe cause mamma always said, "Don't feel bad when they say no, for everyone knows best what he can or cannot do."

I went one day to the dearest old lady (she was older than mamma) and her hair was very white. She put her arm around me and said, "How I wish I could take your paper, but I have not one dollar of my own." I felt bad for her but we visited a little and I sang "Daddy's Tomboy Girl" for her. I only went a little way down the street when I met a very pleasant looking young man and I told him what I was working for. He said, "Well dear, If I had anyone I could send the paper to, I would take it. I want you to get the pony." I said, "Would

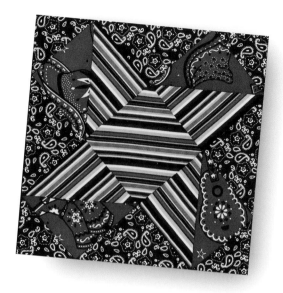

July Fourth (jf)

you truly?" He said, "Yes I would," so I told him about the dear old lady and he gave me 50 cents and said, "Run back and get her name." So you see we were all three happy for that 50 cents; he made both the old lady and me happy and I know he is happier because he did.

I must tell you some of the cute things my pony "Sweetheart" does. One day mamma was picking cherries and "Sweetheart" was around the tree so he knocked the ladder down and mamma had to stay up in the tree for some time until someone came and put the ladder up for her. She scolded "Sweetheart" and told him to go and amuse himself somewhere else, so he chased the chickens until he caught one by the tail. Then he trotted back under the tree mamma was in and held the hen in his mouth and looked up at mamma as much as to say, "This is something new." He does so many cute things.

continued on next page

Lillias and "Sweetheart" Playing Indian

continued

In our town this year we had our big parade at night on the third of July instead of the morning of the Fourth. I rode my "Sweetheart." We were just back of the Grand Marshall and there were bands playing, and fire works. Some of the orders had an elephant and camel and giraffe and other animals made up and dozens of fancy lanterns lighted and carried besides decorated automobiles and all kinds of noises suitable for the Fourth of July, but little "Sweetheart" marched along as though it were nothing unusual and it was the first time he was ever in town after night. There was a big crowd on the streets. You see we are twin cities here. Grass Valley is four miles from Nevada City and we are connected by both electric and steam cars, so one year Nevada City celebrates the Fourth of July and Grass Valley comes with us, the next year we go to Grass Valley and celebrate with them. Mamma says St. Paul and Minneapolis are twin cities too, but I must write about "Sweetheart." Don't you think he was fine to go in that parade and not be afraid, only two years and one month old? Then I had him down again on the Fourth and he saw the flying machine too.

Now for Christmas. "Sweetheart" and I had a fine time. I had a beautiful tree and we had company (both children for me and grownups for mamma and daddy.) In the afternoon of Christmas day we went in the parlor and lit the candles on the tree and there among the many pretty

Christmas Tree (ct)

things hung a pretty tarletan bag with cube sugar in it and apples and tied on with red ribbon were two pretty buttons for his bridle. They are glass with flowers in them and a Christmas card addressed to "Sweetheart." Oh! is not Santa Claus wonderful to remember me and my beautiful pet? When the names were called, mamma opened the door and told "Sweetheart" to come. He walked in through the kitchen and dining room and into the parlor where the company were and up to the tree and looked at the pretty lights. He ate candy and nuts and looked at the people, then daddy told him he must go out. I wish every member of the club and you, Editor, could have seen his sweet black face and bright eyes shining as he stood at the tree and how the children laughed to see him come in the house.

I hope the other members of the club will write and tell me about their little pets.

Best wishes to every Club member and a long prosperous life to our Farmer's Wife.

"ROVER" BROUGHT HAPPINESS TO THIS BRAVE LITTLE CRIPPLED BOY
CLOYD A. RECKART, PRESTON CO., WEST VIRGINIA

My Own Dear Pony "Rover"

I am a crippled boy of 14 years. I have never been able to walk but can read, write and sing.

"Rover" is a great pet with all the little boys and girls around here. He is a great favorite of my dog and they have big times together. My little brothers and sisters are also very fond of him. My sister is just three years old but she rides "Rover" and she looks too cute.

I wouldn't take anything for my dear "Rover." He affords me more pleasure than anything I ever had and I shall always remember you when I am driving my pony and having a good time.

My Own Pony "Jerry" (Part I)

I have the dearest little black Shetland pony named "Jerry" which the Webb Publishing Company sent me free all the way from St. Paul up in Minnesota out here to Lawrence, Kansas.

When I first started out to get my friends to help me win a pony, I can tell you it was pretty hard work. Some of them laughed at me and made fun of me and said: "Oh, you can't win a pony." Sometimes I got a little bit discouraged and at other times I felt sure I was going to win "Jerry." One good old man whom I asked to help me laughed and said he didn't think I would get the pony for he knew of another boy that tried and did not win and that I wouldn't win either. But he gave me his subscription just the same and I told him I would send him a picture of the pony and outfit when I got it which I have done. So you see I had lots of discouraging days, but I also had some pleasant experiences while working in the contest and then came the suspense of waiting to know if I had won or not. It was only a few days, but to me it was ages. So one day my papa and I rode horseback down to the mail box, and I got my precious letter, telling me I had won "Jerry." Oh, I was so excited we just could not make the horse go fast enough, I was so anxious to get back to the house to tell them all that I had really and truly won "Jerry."

After I won "Jerry" I took him on a long trip of eighteen miles to the Annual Old Settler's Meeting at my old home in Oskaloosa, Kansas. My friends were all as enthusiastic over him as I

Kansas (ks)

was, and "Jerry" was proud and showed off his very best. It was a hot day and such crowds that were around us, we could scarcely breathe.

I took "Jerry" down to the Douglas Co. Fair at Lawrence, Kansas, to see if he could win a prize.

There were several other ponies there. One gentleman from Topeka who has a herd of ponies was there with several from his herd, and parties from Lawrence who have more than one pony were there hoping to win both first and second prizes. I took "Captain Jerry" and the buggy down and entered them for the best pony turn-out. We had to compete against both single and double rigs. We were told to drive our ponies out on the race track to show them off and I really believe that "Captain Jerry" knew I wanted him to do his very best for he trotted along so proudly and seemed to know that he was being looked at and admired. I heard one lady say, "O! Look at that darling little black pony" meaning "Captain Jerry." The children all exclaimed to each other and their mammas to look at the little black pony. I believe he knew he was trotting before the judges. Mr. Robertson, a Scotchman, an importer of fine horses, was one of the judges. He admired "Captain Jerry" from the time when he was driven on the track, and when they gave me first prize, $6.00 in cash and tied the blue ribbon on "Captain Jerry" he acted more proud than ever, and how the people in the Grand Stand clapped their hands and cheered.

continued on next page

Cleta Johnson Took First Prize With This Outfit at the Douglas County Fair

105

continued

The gentleman from Topeka, who drove the double rig of Shetland ponies asked me what I would take for my pony. I told him that all the money in the world could not buy him. So many asked me what I gave for the outfit and I told them that I had got it from the Webb Publishing Company, of St. Paul, Minnesota.

One of my friends who helped me in the contest came to me and said, "Cleta you are a lucky little girl to win such a splendid pony and outfit, and to have it win first prize at this Fair." So many of my friends who had helped me during the contest to win "Captain Jerry" were at the Fair and saw and admired him, and they all called him our pony.

I thought I was being well repaid for the work done during the contest in winning "Jerry," and I felt proud, too. I wish all the little girls and boys in the contests could be as lucky as I in winning such a nice little pony that will take me to school or to visit my friends or any place I want to go.

Now I will tell you some of the things "Jerry" likes to eat. He likes so many things that I do not know if I can tell them all. He likes corn better than oats, and likes the corn best on the cob, and that is the way I like it best too when I eat it. We insulted him one day by giving him the shelled corn.

One day he went into the orchard with me for the first time and I went to a tree that had ripe

Pig's Tail (pt)

apples on it and pulled one and gave it to "Jerry" to see if he would eat it, which he did, and then he went to work to help himself, looking on the low limbs and the ground for apples, and ate all he could reach, and would take mine away from me, and take them out of my apron pockets, it was too cunning to see him hunt for them. The next time he went with me to the orchard, as soon as I opened the gate for him he ran just as fast as he could to the very same tree we had

106

visited before, and began to look for apples. If the pigs came around looking for apples, he soon chased them away.

You can see him eating watermelon in the picture. When we are in the yard eating melons he will go from one to another begging for a piece, and if we do not give it to him he will take some-

"Jerry" Eating Watermelon

body's away from them and eat it and he never seems to have quite enough. He often comes to the door and puts his front feet upon the steps and stands with his nose against the screen door looking for me to give him something to eat.

I sometimes take a piece of candy out, and let him find it, which he always does, and looks for more. He is a great lover of sugar, too. One day I let him come in the kitchen and there was a plate on the table with a piece of lemon pie on it, and "Jerry" helped himself to it, and ate it all. When I go out to the barn where he is I always take a piece of bread for him to eat, and he never refuses it, and he dearly loves milk, and will come into the yard and drink every bit we put for the chickens. He likes eggs, too, and sweet potatoes. Really the only thing I have found that he does not like is meat. He loves oranges and peaches and will bite the peaches in two, to get the stones out before eating them. So you see that "Jerry" likes almost any thing that is good to eat, and I like him and the Webb Publishing Company too for giving him to me.

Did I Win a Pony?

*Y*es *I did.* About two years ago I first noticed the offer made by the Webb Publishing Company how I could win a pony. I was willing to enter the contest right away and told my papa about it. He said alright, if you get a half dozen subscriptions all alone, I will try and help you. So I took my sample copy and went to the people to ask them, but when I got there I held my paper in back of me because I was afraid to ask them to subscribe. When I came home papa laughed at me, so I gave it up for that year.

Last year I received a letter from the Pony Editor with an offer of more ponies. When I received this letter I was just wild to get a pony. I started off and got four subscriptions at once, so I kept on working for the pony till the contest closed.

You ought to have seen me a few days later when I received the letter that I had won "Lightning" and his outfit. I could hardly find the door of the post office I was so excited. I ran home all the way and told my parents I had won "Lightning" and how happy we all were. My sister Helen and I went to the depot every day when we thought the pony would come and sure enough the second day we went, the pony came. First they unloaded a red pig and a man said, "There's your pony, Luella," but we waited. Then the baggageman said, "Next a pony,"

Lightning (lg)

"Lightning" Is "Too Cute"

108

and out came "Lightning." As quick as he saw us he began to whinny.

We hardly had him home when almost all the children in the neighborhood were there looking at "Lightning." After the roads got good I gave all my friends a ride and how we did enjoy it.

"Lightning" eats everything we eat. He just loves apples, grapes and watermelons. If we have anything in our hand and call him, he comes running to us. He just loves to play with children and when I go to the barn and leave again, he paws and wants me to stay.

Last June we had to leave our many friends as we moved from Alice, North Dakota. "Lightning" was put in the box car with the other horses and he stood the trip of 275 miles just fine. We soon got better acquainted with our pony here. The first time we hitched up "Lightning," all the little boys and girls ran after us.

About two weeks later it was the Fourth of July and we were asked to go in the parades, so we decorated the buggy and pony and drove in the parade. The children were just wild and parents had to hold them up so they could see better. "Lightning" didn't mind the crackers at all and how proud my sister and I felt.

"Lightning" is so gentle that mamma can trust us to take the baby out riding. We have had many good times with our dear little pony and we would be very lonesome without him. Many people have asked us if we would sell him and how much we want for him, but we won't sell him, he is too cute.

"Lightning" Is So Gentle We Take Baby Out Riding

My name is John Kenyon, I am six years old and was born in the dear old State of Virginia, Co. of Fairfax, where I now live with my papa and mamma. My daddy is a farmer, very fond of good stock, especially good horses and I naturally take after my dad. From the time I was a little tiny boy just large enough to get my legs across a horse's back I have ridden them in from the fields where they have done their day's work and now that I am really able to ride and am getting to be a big boy I have realized my ambition to own a little horse of my own, just as my daddy did when he was given his first driving horses.

When my mamma told me I might enter the pony contest conducted by The Farmer's Wife, goodness how glad I was, and Oh, how hard I did work amongst all our neighbors and friends and the trips I did take way out in the surrounding country to get subscriptions to The Farmer's Wife. My heart used to throb just so hard when I used to think of the good chance I stood of winning "Wizard" and when my mamma received the letter telling me I had won her I was so excited to think I would have a chum and companion such as "Wizard" has proven to be.

My "Wizard" is surely a dandy pony; she is so bright and alert at all times; in fact

Mother's Delight (md)

Look Pleasant, Please

110

mamma thinks she is too alert, for several times she has stolen over to our back porch and drunk the milk which had been put there to cool; and I know my granddaddy, who is in the feed business, has missed a whole lot of feed for when I get on "Wizard" she makes her way to the store and helps herself and when she gets enough she just naturally walks out.

But I know my mamma and granddaddy don't care what "Wizard" takes for they love her as much as I do.

When "Wizard" first came to my house, my dog "Mike," which you see in the picture, was a little bit jealous of her and I don't think "Wizard" liked him very much, but now she has become used to having him around, for everywhere "Wizard" and I go "Mike" goes too, and she seems to miss him if he isn't with us. "Wizard" has many other attractions for me and my daddy and mamma are mighty glad I won her for now I don't have to crowd in the buggy with them

All Aboard!

when they go out but I ride her and she stays right with our horse, too. All of my little friends are great admirers of my pony and I have let them all ride her around the yard, but of course I would not let them go out on the road with her because she might go too fast and spill them off.

I do lots of errands for mamma and daddy and always ride "Wizard." It certainly would make me feel bad to have anything happen to her and I would have to walk again.

I certainly hope more little boys and girls will work as I did and win ponies from The Farmer's Wife, for they are certainly great to have around. The Farmer's Wife is a great paper, too, it not only gives ponies to little boys and girls but it tells them how to take care of them after winning them and then the manager of the Pony department is so kind, if he ever comes to Washington I hope he will come to see "Wizard" and me, for we don't live very far from there.

My Own Dear "Kip"

I want all my friends to know what a lovely pet I now have. When I received the telephone message, telling me that "Kip" had arrived, I just couldn't get to the depot fast enough. Mama, papa and I went right away. They had already taken him out of the crate and he was in a livery barn and, bless his little heart, when he heard us coming he whinnied. It was the sweetest sound to me just then I tell you. Papa put the saddle and bridle on, which came in the morning, and then helped me on his back. A crowd commenced to gather around and all said, "Is that the little pony she got by taking subscriptions for The Farmer's Wife?" We told them yes and wasn't he a little beauty. They all were as excited as I about him.

Miller's Daughter (ml)

On our way home we passed the Fair Grounds where papa has horses in training. All the trainers said he was a fine one and their horses weren't in it with "Kip."

We had a nice box stall waiting for him so we put him in to rest, but I just staid with him till supper time. The next day I commenced to play with him, braiding his lovely mane and tail and brushing him off. A pony is the best playmate a child can have. You ought to see him eat watermelon, cakes, crackers, candy, sugar and fruit. We feed him oats three times a day besides hay and then when in pasture he gets all the clover and grass he wants. I haven't

"Kip" and Anna Ruth Eating Lunch

had him long enough to teach him many tricks. He shakes hands and rubs his velvety nose on you after you give him anything.

He is growing more beautiful than ever. Although I am so young, I can hitch and unhitch him and do everything for him. I want to do all for him myself, he is so gentle and kind. My first thought in the morning is of my darling, what good times we will have together. Sometimes I drive home alone if papa isn't quite ready to come. We only live about half mile from Fair Grounds but I pass a great many autos and other vehicles. I have always been used to horses so that I have no fear about driving alone. I always keep to the right and then you are all right. One feels safe with a little pony, as they are not afraid of anything. One of the pictures shows me in my little racing cart.

If every girl and boy wanted a pony as much as I did, they certainly would join The Farmer's Wife Pony Club and try to get one. Don't let anyone try to discourage you by saying there isn't anything in it, but keep right on getting all the subscribers you can and I assure you the Webb Publishing Company will do all they can for you to get a pony. Everything they promise to do they will most assuredly keep their word. I shall never forget their kindness to me all through the contest and will always try to get them subscribers whenever I can.

I must close now for when I get talking about my dear little "Kip," I never know when to stop. I send kind wishes to all my little unknown friends and hope you all will join The Farmer's Wife Pony Club and be as happy as I am.

"I Drive 'Kip' Around the Race Track in My Little Cart"

I am sending you some pictures of my pony, "Pilot." I live a long way from a town so I did not have any chance to have his picture taken before. We live close to a high range of mountains, which is covered with thick forests, and my papa is a forest ranger. He rides all through the woods looking out for fires or timber thieves and seeing that the nursery work is getting along well. It is bully work and I enjoy going with him up into the forest on "Pilot." My papa fixed me a little ax and a saddle bag just like his and I help him on his work. "Pilot" is nice and gentle. I can turn him loose and catch him any place. I drive the cows and horses in from the pasture with him. I ride him to school and all my schoolmates have ridden him. They all like him as well as I do. Nearly every Sunday I have a lot of kids come to see "Pilot" and ride him; he is so gentle that three small kids can ride at a time. I can drive him, too, but I like to ride him the best.

Now, I must tell you how I won "Pilot." I have a nice driving dog—his name is Prince—and I drove him nearly every day for about 5 weeks getting subscribers to the paper. I worked hard and so did my dog, but I promised my dog that if I could win "Pilot" I

Mountain Maze (mm)

"Pilot" and Freddie in the Mountains

would give him a rest and so I have. I am sending you a picture of my good dog and cart and hope you will have room for it in "Lucky Pony Winners," because I couldn't have won "Pilot" without him.

All the people that took the paper like it fine and say it is a very good paper. I have a little stable for "Pilot" where I keep him by himself. We have lots of good hay and oats and I take the very best care of him. I turn him into the field when I think he needs a little green grass. I rode him down to the city of Townsend and my Dad and Uncle Steve helped me to trim him up and I rode him in the parade on the 4th of July. We caused great excitement and some of the people said "Pilot" was the whole thing. Well, Mr. Pony Man, I cannot say enough in praise of "Pilot." He is just the dearest pony that ever happened. He eats apples, candy and bread and drinks milk.

Well, I could write all day about "Pilot," but I suppose you don't want too long a letter, so I'll close by thanking you 1,000 times for this fine outfit.

We Caused Great Excitement in the Parade

When I first started to get subscriptions to win my pony, it was funny to hear the different people's opinions. One man would say, "Oh, you won't get anything; you are just wasting your time, so I won't take the paper." Others would say, "You must work like everything and show them what a Brookings Co. boy can do." Several took the paper for five years and nearly all the rest for two years. The first person to help was my school teacher. I sent in my last list of subscriptions the 25th day of May, 1912, and very anxiously waited to hear the winner's name. On the morning of the 28th I received a telephone message that I was the winner of "Buster."

You can't begin to imagine how tickled my two brothers and sister and I were. We danced around as if we were crazy, jumping over chairs and we even upset a big can of floor paint. I went to Elkton (we live six miles from the town) the evening of the 28th and was very much disappointed when he did not arrive. Neither did he come on the 29th, so we left word with the drayman, that when he came he should take

Everybody's Favorite (ev)

"Will You Have Lemonade, 'Buster?'"

him out of his crate and let me know. "Buster" arrived in Elkton the 30th of May at about four o'clock in the morning. The drayman took him home with him and took him right in the bedroom where his little girl was asleep. She always calls him her pony. I went up after him that forenoon and rode him home. We are all in love with "Buster." He is crazy for apples, sugar, salt, and eats ice cream, bananas and bread, too.

"Buster" just loves to run races. When I first got him my father thought he could run faster than "Buster" could because he was so small, so we ran a race and I beat him a long way. If a buggy or wagon comes up behind me when I have him hitched he won't let it go by and if an auto goes around us, he runs as fast as he can to try to catch it, but he can't go quite as fast as an automobile.

When I take my pony, "Buster," to town everyone on the street says, "Oh! Look at that cute little pony." They all think it so strange that he hauls such a large load so easily.

I got my pony a year ago today and I am sure I think a great deal more of him now than I did then. Why, I would not take three hundred dollars for him. He is so cute and smart. If I go out in the pasture and call, "Come Buster," he will come running up to me, but sometimes when he thinks I want to drive him, he won't let me catch him for quite a while. Sometimes we turn him out in the yard and then he comes to the door two or three times a day to get an apple. Then when he has eaten the apple, he goes away and starts eating grass until he gets hungry for another apple. He eats peaches and plums too and spits out the seeds just like a boy or girl and he just loves to drink milk. When he is standing in the barn if you ask him if he wants some oats he will nod his head. I don't know what we would do without "Buster." He hauls a case of eggs and some butter and one or two of us children to Ward twice a week. You know I live on a farm. I drove him to school all winter. We have two miles to go and he

continued on page 119

"Everyone Says, 'Oh! Look at That Cute Little Pony'"

117

We had moved on a farm 10 miles from Aitkin, Minn., just a few weeks, when one day I didn't know what to do. I was so lonesome as I have no sisters or brothers and had left all my little friends and hadn't made any new acquaintances. I picked up a copy of a farm paper and was looking through it when I saw where the Webb Publishing Company was going to give away a Shetland pony to any boy or girl who was willing to work. As I had always wanted a pony, I asked papa to let me try to win one. He said, "Alright, but you don't stand much of a chance to win as everybody is strangers to us." But I could not give up the idea so I sent in my name to the Pony Editor at St. Paul, Minn., and in a few days I got a letter telling what to do, so I went to work in earnest.

I had no trouble getting subscribers as I got them on the merit of the paper, but no one thought I would win, but I just kept on working the harder and when I got my letter telling me I had won "Scout" and the outfit, I believe it was the happiest day of my life. I began planning the good times "Scout" and I would have. I had a long anxious wait before "Scout" came but he was only that much dearer to me when he did come.

"Scout" just loves to be petted. He seems to be happy when I am

Minnesota (mn)

All Ready for a Ride

with him and will come to me when I call. He likes almost anything to eat that I give him and is exceptionally fond of cake and sugar. I have had several chances to sell "Scout" at a good price but wouldn't sell him at any price for I never get lonesome any more since "Scout" came to live with me, for when I don't know what else to do, I saddle my pony and go for a ride. Mamma and I drive "Scout" to Sunday School almost every Sunday and Papa is going to build me a little barn at the school house and I am going to ride to school this year.

I can never thank the Webb Publishing Company enough for "Scout" and his outfit.

Lucinda and Friends With "Scout"

"BUSTER"

continued from page 117

hauls four of us to school every day and did not mind at all. I have looked carefully at all the pictures in the "Lucky Pony Winners" but I cannot find any pony that looks as good to me as "Buster" does, and if any boy or girl really wants a pony I advise them to write the Webb Publishing Company right away. They are so honest and do just exactly everything they promise and I certainly thank them a thousand times for my pony, "Buster."

119

My little sister Agnes and I were reading a farm paper one evening last winter, and we saw down in one corner, "A pony given away by the Webb Publishing Co. just by working for The Farmer's Wife Pony Club."

To me that seemed an easy way to get a pony. But when I asked papa and mamma they said they did not think I would win a prize, that it would mean lots of work and they tried to discourage me, but they let me try.

I tell you the names of my friends came like snow-flakes to my mind and I wrote and asked them to take "The Farmer's Wife," telling them of the value of the paper to them and the wonderful prize to me. Just a few laughed and said I would get no pony after my hard work.

I joined the Pony Club and every time I would send in a list of names they would write me such a nice letter. That encouraged me a great deal and I could imagine the pony here and all mine long before she came.

In the middle of June, I went to the station with our man, to mail something. The postmaster said, "Master William, here is a parcel just for you." Why, there was my saddle and bridle. No one knows how delighted I was, for if that had come, then I knew my pony must be on her way. Sure enough my mamma got a letter saying that we might expect "Mayflower" on the third of July. I tell you I was glad my order for fire-works had gone in, for I could hardly keep my mind on the "Good Old Fourth."

Mayflower (my)

I cannot tell you how delighted I was when I got a telephone call from the express man that my pony was really there. My little sister and I hustled off for the station, each with lumps of sugar in our pockets. We talked to big brother about the pony, all the way, so that the way would seem short. How delighted I was when I saw "Mayflower"—the pony I own!

We children were not the only happy ones, but the whole family and neighbors gave us a happy

120

welcome—in fact the flags came out the day before the Fourth.

On the way home, what do you think, a man wanted to buy her, but "Mayflower" was not for sale. Before we reached home we were quite well acquainted.

I tell you she was glad to get out of the crate for she had come all the way from St. Paul. I had a box-stall ready for her, but the lawn and all the children took her eye.

She has a beautiful chestnut colored head with a white star on her forehead, chestnut hip, white back and flank, and a handsome chestnut mane and tail. I cannot tell you how fine she is. Last summer she took first prize at the Co. fair and I was very proud of her.

I cannot thank the Webb Pub. Co. enough for sending me such a wonderful prize.

Bringing Up the Cows

I'll tell you how it was. About May 1st, I found your advertisement about "Winkle" and his dandy outfit saying, "Send us your name if you want him for your own." I read it all over and over and wished to enter the contest. I wanted to work for him. I asked papa over and over to let me try, but he was busy all the time and didn't listen to me.

Finally I persuaded him and one of my uncles to give me their subscriptions so I could become a member and after I received my blanks, etc., I went to work in earnest and mailed my first list on May 12th. I worked hard every day till the 29th of June, being less than two months. I went to a little town fourteen miles away with the mail man and got a number of subscriptions. I was almost a little stranger there, but I had a good friend that went with me to many places. I had a good time as it was good fun working for "Winkle." Everyone was kind to me and after I came home, my uncle went with me around in the neighboring section. One of my aunts made trips with me and I had a nice time on all of my trips and around home I did not let anyone pass or miss anyone without giving them a chance to subscribe for The Farmer's Wife and help me to win a pony. It was wonderful. Scarcely anyone ever turned me down and I feel so thankful to them for their

North Carolina Beauty (nc)

Why Shouldn't I Be Happy?

122

kindness, but of course I found a few cranky people and I guess all of our Pony Club Members did too, but I didn't get discouraged.

When I received your good letter, telling me I had won "Winkle," I just leaped for joy and clapped my hands. I ran to the telephone and told my aunt I had won "Winkle" and his outfit and she was so overjoyed she ran about one-half mile across a cornfield to break the news to grandpa about my success. Aunt is a large fleshy woman and just imagine how funny she looked running across the cornfield to break the news to grandpa. And when she told him he threw down his hoe and up with his hat and called to my uncle and said, "We will stop right where we are and do no more work today, but will go over and spend the evening with Myrtle Pearl and sit up with her tonight, for I know she won't sleep any." So on they came and several of my friends came too and we had a regular jubilee.

But the best of all was on June 9th. The mail man was at the station when "Winkle" came in. He led him out and on to my home that evening 14 miles distant. When he got to the post office is where the true happiness was expressed. I was so happy I almost cried. I hugged "Winkle's" neck, talked to him and we were perfect friends from the very beginning. He is so good and kind.

continued on page 125

"Winkle" and Myrtle Pearl After the Mail

I am a little girl twelve years old, four feet and ten inches tall. I weigh about eighty pounds and have dark hair and light eyes. My pony "Judy" is forty-two inches high and nearly three years of age. His color is dark brown and he weighs close to three hundred pounds.

We were looking for him a few days before he came, and finally he arrived one Sunday. I got a telephone call that my pony was at the depot, but we could not come down that night, so the depot agent put him into the livery barn until the next morning, we came down after him, and he was so cute everybody came to see him. We could hardly come out of town because the children all were so anxious to see a little Shetland pony— and grown persons, too. All the people said he was just like a little sheep because he still had his woolly coat on. Some people asked me how much I wanted for him, then I said, "No, I won't sell him at any price." When we went home my little brother Willie led him and he kept up with our two horses all the six miles out of town. When we reached home my other three brothers said, "Oh! isn't he little!"

"Judy" likes to be around other horses, but he does not go very close to them for he knows he might get a kick from them any time.

In the mornings when papa gets up he looks in the barn and "Judy" is always asleep, then he calls "Judy" and he just makes one jump and there he is by the window whinnying to get out.

Quite often the neighbors come to play with

Next Door Neighbor (nd)

"Judy" and me. "Judy" makes me feel happy all the time now, and I am never going to sell him.

The best thing "Judy" likes to do is to go into the house and get some sugar and water, and he likes cheese awfully well. The first thing he does when he goes into the house is to go to the table

On Dress Parade

and get something to eat. But he just hates to go out of the house.

He will be awfully pretty when he has shed off, his color will be black and his legs kind of brown, and his mane and tail are so long and pretty.

I surely do thank the Webb Publishing Co. for the dandy pony they gave me.

HOW "WINKLE" WAS WON
continued from page 123

Little friend, if you want a pony for your own, don't delay in entering the contest. The Webb Publishing Company certainly will treat you right. The outfit, pony and all is much better than I had ever imagined. Do not doubt or feel discouraged. The contest is absolutely fair and you will get all that is coming to you. I have had so many letters of congratulation from my dear little Pony Club Members. Am so glad to get in touch with so many dear little friends.

I am only 11 years old and live among the mountains of North Carolina where people are not very thickly settled, so most of the little boys and girls have a better chance than I did. So no one need to feel discouraged on entering the contest. It will be an easy victory.

*M*y pony *"Hummer"* arrived Saturday the 25th on the 11:20 Express, and received a warm reception. I think he is a very fine little pony, and fulfills all your descriptions of him. "Hummer" is surely the right name for him, for he is a clever little hummer.

Received the handsome bridle and saddle, and they certainly look fine on him. The horse-hair bridle has been a curiosity among the neighborhood, and greatly admired.

"Hummer" is just as fine as ever. He weighed three hundred and fifty pounds including the crate when I received him. Now he weighs four hundred and seventy pounds without the crate, so by that he must be well contented.

I take drives and go saddle riding with "Hummer" very often. We certainly have fine times together.

I cannot thank The Farmer's Wife enough for my pony "Hummer." He is the sweetest pony I know of anywhere. I was so happy the day I heard I had won him that I couldn't sleep that night. I am sure I was the happiest boy in town.

"Hummer" knows me in a large crowd and I have taught him several tricks. Every morning when I go down to see him he kisses and shakes hands with me. We have a pasture for "Hummer" and when we go to the bars and call him he will come running every time. Along side the fence in the pasture field is a peach tree which hangs over the fence. "Hummer" used to go to the tree and reach for the peaches. After he had

New Jersey (nj)

eaten all the meat off, he would spit the stone out.

One morning early "Hummer" pushed the bars down and got out. I didn't know anything about it till one of our neighbors said they were going to send me a feed bill because they found "Hummer" in their barn standing at the feed box eating. Every time he has gotten out since then, he tries to get to the same place.

I have been advised by a good horseman that he is a fine pony and not to sell him under two hundred and fifty dollars, but I told him that money would never buy him. I never have had him out but what there have been people to tell me I had a sweet little pony. I thank The Farmer's Wife over and over again for the way they have treated me.

"The Sweetest Pony I Know of Anywhere"

Before I commence telling you about my dear little pony, "Bunny," let me introduce myself, so that you may know who I am and where I live. I am a little red headed Norwegian boy and was 10 years old on June 17th. I live with my parents, four sisters and two brothers on a 40-acre farm on the banks of the Red River of the North, three miles west from the village of Climax, Polk Co., Minnesota.

Last summer I saw an advertisement in a paper that the Webb Publishing Company of St. Paul, Minn., was giving away ponies to little boys and girls. As I had always wanted a pony that I could call my own, I asked my mamma and papa if they would let me try and win a pony. They said I could try but papa said he thought I would not succeed. Anyhow I entered the contest and began to get subscribers. I found it very easy as almost everyone said they would take the paper as they thought it was the best farm paper in the state. After school and on Saturdays, I would get papa's horse and buggy and sometimes mamma would go with me and I would start out working, and I kept on until the last hour of the contest, all the time being confident that I would win "Bunny."

As "Bunny" was intended for a Christmas present the winner would be notified Christmas Eve. Arriving home from school Christmas Eve, no notice had arrived and mamma and papa both said that I had lost. I could hardly keep the tears back, as I had worked so hard and been so

Norway Pine (np)

sure all the time that I would have the happiest Christmas in my life. I was just getting ready to retire for the night, much sadder than usual and wondering who the lucky winner of "Bunny" could be. Listen! Somebody knocking at the door! Mamma went and opened the door. Here was Uncle Ole and one of our neighbors. They told mamma that I was the lucky winner of the little pony and outfit, as they had been informed over the phone that the buggy had arrived that evening. I fairly jumped out of bed and dressed faster than I ever did before and ran out to greet

Uncle and asked him if it was really true that I had won "Bunny." He assured me that it was and that I now had a pony and buggy of my own.

continued on next page

"I Use 'Bunny' on the Cultivator"

continued

I am unable to describe here how happy I felt. I doubt very much if the English language contains words whereby I could describe it, if I should try. Anyhow, they are not at my command. Oh! I was so happy. Mamma, papa, my sisters and brothers were so happy too.

We drove to town that night and arrived there just as the train pulled in from the North. "Bunny" was not on the train, but as papa had told me that if I won "Bunny" he would come on the morning train, I was sure he would come Christmas morning. We loaded the buggy, harness and saddle into the sled and went home. Early next morning, papa, mamma, uncle and myself drove up town and sure enough there was "Bunny" standing on the depot platform. I felt so sorry for him as the morning was very cold. We soon had him in Uncle's sled and started for home. As soon as I got home, I took him in the house and gave him a little water and some sugar and cookies and made a nice warm place for him in the barn. So after all I had the happiest Christmas in my life.

The first time I hitched him to the buggy, he did not know just what it meant, but papa led him around a little and he became very quiet at once. I can now drive him anywhere as he is not afraid of anything. If we meet an auto, he don't seem to notice it. I go horseback after the cows and use him on the cultivator, cultivating

John's Favorite (jo)

mamma's garden. He is so careful not to step on any plants. He is everybody's pet as he is the only real Shetland pony here. I shall never sell him as long as he lives.

Thanking you from the bottom of my heart for sending me "Bunny" and the outfit and also for your fair treatment and thanking everybody who so willingly subscribed for the paper and assisted in making me the happiest boy that ever lived, I remain, yours for success, Jno. M. Borsvold.

"On the Banks of the Red River of the North"

MY DARLING LITTLE PET
CHARLIE MAHONEY, CHIPPEWA CO., MICHIGAN

"Peter" steals the clothes pins out of my mother's basket while she is hanging out the clothes. He will pick them up one at a time with his teeth and if she doesn't watch him he will pick the clothes up out of the basket and let them fall on the ground. But mama never gets mad at "Peter" no matter what he does and, of course, we all think it is cute.

My North "Star"

I received "Star" June 2nd and papa and I went to town to get him. We had him in the wagon box in the crate and took him home with the oxen, which you will see in the picture.

"Star" is a pretty, brown Shetland pony, three years old and forty-one inches tall and very cute. So many told me when I told them that I was trying to win a Shetland pony by getting subscribers for the paper that I would get a picture of a pony and buggy and some thought that I would not get anything, but they all think different now. There have been so many here to see my rig and they all think it the cutest in the neighborhood. My friends say they will also try to get a rig like mine if the Webb Publishing Company has any more contests.

"Star" just loves a dish of strawberries and also likes oats and sugar.

My folks think my rig the best present I could have gotten and don't know when I ever would have owned a pony of my own if it had not been for the Webb Publishing Company of St. Paul.

When my friends come, we hitch up "Star" and go out driving and they all think it lots of fun. One Sunday when quite a few of my friends were here, we took "Star" on top of an old straw stack and had our pictures taken.

North Star (ns)

"We Took 'Star' Home With the Oxen"

He is not afraid of automobiles and will go right up and look at them.

So many say they cannot understand how the Webb Publishing Company can give away so much for so little work but they do and every child ought to try for one because they are the best ponies that children could have.

One day my friends and sisters were going out to pick strawberries and we had our lunches with us and "Star" took a good load of us there and he seemed to enjoy it as much as any of us and ate almost as many strawberries as any of us did.

Again I thank you for "Star" and all you sent me.

"There's Always Room at the Top"

*O*ne evening last winter we sat reading by the table. In my paper I saw an advertisement stating the Webb Publishing Company would give away free a Shetland Pony, so mother suggested my trying to get it. So that evening I wrote them I would like to try for it and within a few days I received a reply and went to work.

The first day I got 12 subscriptions and that encouraged me most wonderfully, but some days I did not do so well as others and would get discouraged, but father and mother would say, "Don't give up. You stand as good a chance as the rest." So I would keep right on and every little while the Webb Publishing Company would send me an encouraging letter which helped very much. Finally the contest closed and then came the anxious days of waiting to see who had won. But my folks did not tell me I had won a special pony until it arrived at the station. She did not look so nice at first but she looked very cute to me and in a few days came the saddle and bridle which would please most any boy and then I learned to ride her.

One day as I was currying her I noticed some mites in her mane so we clipped her and got rid of them and she has gained very rapidly ever since.

As my pony was young when she came, I favored her at first but she is now older and does anything I ask of her. I gave her a nice little white leather halter and some chocolate candy for a birthday present.

New York (ny)

I drive my pony to school which is in town and about 1½ miles away. I take her grain with me and at noon when I go in the barn to feed her she always asks for it. I feed her nearly two quarts of whole oats a day and an ear of corn night and morning. How she does love to run and play in the field when I turn her out to eat grass. You would be surprised to see how fast she can run.

All of my little friends thinks she is just fine and would like her for their very own. Everyone seems to admire her as she is the only one around here.

Now, let me tell you what the Webb Publishing Company did for me to show you how honest and fair they were with me. When my parents learned I had won a pony they had heard me say I would like a black mare pony, so they wrote to the Webb Publishing Company and they did not have one on hand at that time so they sent to another pony farm in Illinois and she was shipped to me from there. So I certainly think they have used me fine and I thank them a thousand times for their special efforts to please me, for they did as they agreed and more all through the contest.

I have had lots of chances to sell my pony. Before she was taken out of the crate at the station, a man wanted to buy her for his children. The first day I drove her to town I was offered $150.00. She took first premium at our Co. Fair this season.

Hoping the Webb Publishing Company will continue to give away more ponies so other boys and girls can get one I will close with best wishes to all Pony Club Members and the Webb Pub. Co.

"Special Delivery Wagon"

My Pony "Evangeline"

It' would be nice to have a pony and now that I really have one that the Webb Publishing Company gave me I find that it is much nicer than I ever imagined. I know if you ever get a pony that you will feel the same way about it as I do about my "Evangeline." All the boys and girls in our town think almost as much of "Evangeline" as I do and I can't begin to tell all of the good times I have had with her, I have had so many since she came.

I couldn't begin to tell you all the adventures I have had when out driving. Once I got stuck in the mud and "Evangeline," my pony, pulled me out, and then another time when coming home we got on the wrong road and we didn't know what to do until we remembered reading that horses always knew the way home so we let "Evangeline" have the reins and she brought us safely home.

One day some girls came by in their pony cart and my brother and I went driving with them and had lots of fun. My pony will carry double and my brother takes all of his friends riding, so do I. Sometimes when it is nice I get up early and go out horse-back riding before breakfast and when a girl is spending the night with me we both go and that's more fun. Sometimes we play Indian and dress up in our Indian suits and ride "Evangeline" bare back like real Indians.

Old Indian Trail (ot)

Sitting Pretty

136

I find "Evangeline" very useful and what do you think, she is really making me rich. You see the Webb Publishing Company really gave me two ponies. First they sent "Evangeline" to me in October and then one morning in April, Dan, the hired man, called Mamma and said a little stranger was at the barn. You can imagine my surprise and delight to find that "Evangeline" had the dearest little colt. We gave her the name of "Beauty." Pony colts are worth stacks of money so that's one way I am getting rich. Then I showed "Evangeline" at our Fair and won first premium with her. I also run all kinds of errands with her. Sometimes my papa sends me to town to get him cigars and he always pays me for it, and my mamma sends me just lots of times to buy groceries, and she pays me too. Then my grandma gave me an old rubber hose and lots of rags and I took them to the ragman with my pony and cart and he bought them from me. My uncle has a farm near our town and one day last winter he wanted to go out there to see about some cattle and pigs he had and he didn't have any way to go. You see we always send our horses away every winter and so does he, so he didn't have any horse to drive and it was too muddy for an auto. So what do you suppose he did? He hired "Evangeline" my pony, and she took him out there in just a little while.

I know I could hire "Evangeline" out to boys and girls for so much an hour and then I'd get rich quick for they are all crazy about her, but I am not going to because I am afraid some of them might be unkind to her and that would break my heart for I love her so.

Gladys and Marshall Houx and "Evangleine" and Her Colt, "Beauty"

137

I want to say a few words about my dear pony "Pansy." She is the dearest little pony that could be had. She came from the only true publishing company in the world so she cannot help being true to me. She is so kind to me in every way, like the publishers of The Farmer's Wife, who gave me everything that they said they would give. And so my dear little pony will do anything I wish her to do. When I hitch her to the little buggy I have as pretty an outfit as anyone. My aunt gave me a nice robe to make my outfit complete. My parents are well pleased with my outfit and feel proud of my little pony when my little sister and I ride out.

I think every boy and girl ought to have a pony and outfit to be happy and it shows too that they have tried to do something to help others and, at the same time, helps them to a great pleasure. When I think of being the owner of such a fine pony, I feel that I cannot thank the Webb Publishing Company and the Pony Editor enough and also my friends who helped me to get it and who praise The Farmer's Wife for such a nice paper.

I must tell you of some of the cute things my pony does. When she goes into her pasture every morning she looks for apples. She takes a straight line to each tree unless she sees our flock of geese around a tree. She then will go there first and drive them away. She will drive our dog out of her pasture too, and when I go to see her at any time she will look my pockets over for cake.

Pansy (pa)

There were thimble berries in her pasture and when I went to pick them she would follow me and eat them when I was trying to pick and get her nose in my pail.

Some mornings papa lets her out of the barn and she trots to the house and comes up the steps and knocks at the door with her nose. And when ever she comes to the door there is a little white chicken that comes with her to eat the crumbs "Pansy" drops when eating cake. It seems cute that the little chicken knows just when to come.

My "Pansy" dearly loves apples, cake, sugar, candy and ice cream and many other things.

Sometimes when I water her with a pail, if she does not want to drink she will tip it over with her foot. She will kiss my face and hands and root me around with her little nose when I don't have her cake ready before she starts to the pasture. I would not sell her for any amount for I should be so lonely without her, she is such a dear little friend. She will come into the house and eat off the table and make herself quite at home with us, the same as one of the family.

Now I wish to say to all my little friends, do not hesitate to join the Pony Club and do not let anyone discourage you but just place confidence in the Webb Publishing Company for they stand back of every word and promise they make you. They are true hearted and whole hearted or they would never give so many ponies away to make the children so happy and cheer our little hearts as they do when we receive one of their dear little ponies to be our very own. I could say more, but I must leave room for some other little boy or girl to tell of his good luck.

I will close with best wishes to you and all the children who read my story and look at my pictures, and I would like to have any of them write me or exchange pictures. I will thank you once more, but cannot express my feelings toward the Webb Publishing Company for what they have done for me.

"Sister Enjoys My Pony With Me"

*O*ne *dreary February* evening I felt lonely and tired after sitting all day in an invalid chair, for I was just getting over a spell of sickness and was still too weak to take exercise. I was waiting for papa to come and carry me back to my room upstairs. I had been amusing myself by looking at some pictures of ponies in a catalogue, and felt rather blue about getting one, for they were so very high priced, and I feared I might never have one all my own.

When supper was over papa took me on his back, pony fashion, and gave me a jolly ride up the stairs. Then I wanted to talk to him about getting me a real live pony that I could ride and drive when the Springtime came, so I might grow strong and well like other girls and boys.

After we had talked awhile I suddenly remembered that grandmother read something that day about a pony contest, and I told papa of it. He said, "I don't believe in such things much but get the paper and I'll see what it's about anyway." Mamma made a search for the paper and soon we were all eagerly reading about "Mac" and the complete pony outfit to be given away by the Webb Publishing Company. The more we read of "Mac" the more anxious we were to try and win him.

When the contest closed I waited anxiously to hear from it, and time went slowly for I was again confined to my bed. But one morning just as I awoke papa came into my room with a broad smile on his face and a yellow slip in his hand,

Patience Corners (pc)

which said, "Ruth wins Mac." I never was quite so happy in my life, and three nights later I received the largest express package I ever expect to get, "Mac." He was escorted down the street from the station by about 30 men and boys, and as he walked proudly along he seemed to feel that such attention was only due him.

I was too sick to ride or drive him for several days after he came, but as soon as I was strong enough I rode him about the yard, and I shall never forget my first drive to town with my little chum. We hitched "Mac" to my beautiful little cart, and we drove through town and down Main street we attracted as much attention as if we had been a circus parade, for it was the only pony outfit in town. Men, women and children came out and stood all along the street, to look at "Mac" and pet him, and how proud I did feel of him.

I have no brothers or sisters to enjoy "Mac" with me, but I have lots of little friends who are always ready for a ride or a drive. "Mac" is fond of eating out of my hand and loves candy and cake. One day as I was driving down Main street near the popcorn stand, he suddenly walked up to a crowd of men and put his nose into a bag of popcorn one of them was holding. Of course they all laughed and fed him all they had, but "Mac" did not forget it, and for a long time he wanted to stop at the pop corn stand every time he went to town.

I have simply lived in the fresh air, playing with my pony, and have grown quite strong and well again, and think "Out Door Life With Mac" was the best medicine I ever had.

Now if you don't believe me,
Just stop off at Slater and see,
The dearest little black pony,
And a girl as strong as can be.

Going on a Picnic With "Mac"

141

*W*hile looking over some papers one cold wintry evening in the fall, we noticed where many ponies had been given to children all over the United States by the Webb Publishing Company of St. Paul, Minnesota.

We at once read the ad over carefully and began trying to convince our parents that we could win a pony if others could. We filled out the blank in the paper and sent it to the Webb Publishing Company as they wished us to do.

In about a week the required material with which to work came, and we at once started to get subscriptions for "The Farmer's Wife."

We began by asking the neighbors nearest home before and after school. Papa gave us an old broncho to ride and we took turns at going out.

As brother was only eight and myself ten years of age we had to be home by dark, but by so doing we soon had our first subscription blank of twenty subscribers filled out.

How proud and encouraged we felt over our first blank we sent in, and after this getting subscribers was not hard at all.

Friends everywhere were very kind and began to be very much interested in our work. We met with few discouragements and do

Pleasant Paths (pp)

Vera, "Gus" and Frank

not know how to express our appreciation of the kindness shown us.

After doing all we could near home before and after school, I realized that in order to win "Gus," I must work hard every day and not leave a day pass without getting some new subscribers.

As taking subscriptions seemed to be a great schooling to me, I did not regret so much my having to miss several days of school work. While canvassing, I became acquainted with all the nearby towns; I learned the lay of the country and also learned much by writing continually, the work which is required of a contestant.

Much knowledge is obtained also by meeting people of different classes. Before entering the contest, I hardly knew one piece of silver from another, but now can make change with any one in silver or paper. Since winning "Gus," I have received dozens of letters and of course in answering them have learned much about letter writing.

The schooling alone was worth the time and energy spent even if I had not won a pony.

Many a cold stormy day found me out canvassing, for the old saying is, "Work Before Pleasure."

continued on next page

"One Day We Led 'Gus' Right Into an Automobile"

143

continued

After waiting anxiously for four days after the contest closed, a telegram came from the Webb Publishing Co., St. Paul, Minn., saying we had won "Gus."

Now came pleasure after work. What joy at home and what a happy bunch of children!

We were overcome with joy while receiving the telegram and quickly phoned the news to our kind friends and schoolmates. Within a week our dear little "Gus" arrived and brother and I went seven miles to the depot to meet him.

We cannot tell you half the pleasure there is in owning a Shetland pony, and no child who works for one and wins will ever begrudge the time and energy spent.

"Gus" is very useful as well as a pleasure. We go to Sunday-school and take music lessons with him and do many errands for papa and mamma. Taking the cows to pasture and bringing them home at night is a great help on the farm.

"Gus" is also full of tricks. He will lie down and go to sleep while we sit on him, jump the rope while I ride him, take lead pencils out of a man's pocket, come into the house to get a drink, eat sugar or anything good out of my hands, whinny when he sees us children coming home from school, turn the door knob to get into the house, and do many tricks which I have not time or space

Friendship Star (fs)

to mention. And one day we led him right into an automobile.

It is hard for me to bring a story to a close when it is about my Shetland pony, but I must do so.

In conclusion, I wish to thank the Webb Publishing Co. for their honesty, kindness and promptness in answering the many letters which I had to send them during the pony competition. Never shall I forget them.

THE WEBB PUBLISHING COMPANY

WHO WE ARE

The Webb Publishing Company was founded in 1883 and is the largest agricultural publishing house west of New York City. We print annually more than sixteen million copies of our two agricultural periodicals. We also publish many agricultural books. Any bank or business house in St. Paul or Minneapolis will tell of the high

standing of the Webb Publishing Company and that every promise we make will be faithfully carried out.

OUR NATIONAL MAGAZINE

The Farmer's Wife is a monthly magazine for farm women and farm homes, and it is the only magazine of its kind published in America. Its monthly circulation of 750,000 copies is exceeded by but few periodicals of any kind.

There is a department for every side of home-making and home-keeping: Interesting Stories, Tested Recipes, Smart Patterns, Latest Fancy Work Designs, Garden Hints, Poultry Pointers, Rural Club Activities and many others.

The subscription price is only 50 cents for three years and we will gladly send a sample copy free upon request.

—from the 1915 *Lucky Pony Winner* booklet

Webb Publishing Company's Three Big Office Buildings
55 to 79 East Tenth St., St. Paul, Minn.

I want to tell you and all inquiring friends how pleased I am with my pony and outfit. When the time came for the pony to come my brother and Papa and I went to the depot to meet him but when the train came in no pony, and we kept this up for two nights. Everybody said my pony would not come, but I knew he would and sure enough on the third night when the train rolled in the express man opened the door to the car. I heard a pony neigh and how tickled I was for there he was in the crate all decorated with ribbons on his tail and mane. Then a little later the saddle, bridle and harness and rest of the outfit came by express.

Then when snow came Papa made a cutter and so you can see us in the picture with "Sportsman," that is my pony's name, hitched up. We ride him and drive him all over and when we turn him out to play he will come to the dining room door and want to come in. One day I led him in the dining room and we had just finished breakfast and he walked up to the table and ate the crumbs off baby sister's plate. He is just as gentle as a kitten and very kind to us. He eats apples, candy and anything you give him. "Sportsman" is so gentle that we can do anything with him and he is a trick pony and can do 21 different tricks. He will tell how old he is by pawing with his foot, lie down and let you get on and then get up, roll over, stand on his hind feet, shake hands, etc., but I don't want to take up so much room

Ribbons (rb)

telling you his tricks that I can't tell you of my joy and I am so happy to think that I've got a Shetland Pony all my own.

Anybody that works for the Webb Publishing Company will certainly get paid for their work. When I started to get subscriptions for their paper everybody told me I would not get enough to get a pony, but I just kept going and now I have got my pony and he is a dandy and I have the Webb Publishing Company to thank for all my generous treatment. I will be glad to correspond with anyone personally in regard to their reliability.

I will close with best wishes to all who try for ponies from the Webb Publishing Co., also to the Webb Publishing Co., who made it possible for me to have a pony.

"Papa Made Us a Cutter"

*R*ob Roy is a dandy little fellow the Webb Publishing Company gave me for winning in the Pony Club. They gave away lots of ponies to the girls and boys, and I stood second. My, but I was surprised when I got the letter stating that I had won so close to first; I thought I would come in about fifteenth or twentieth.

When mamma and I first started in getting subscriptions for The Farmer, the most welcome paper that comes to our house, my friends would try and discourage us. One man said, "You won't get a pony because my boy tried to win one. It's too hard work." We asked if he tried from the Webb Publishing Company. He said, "No." Another man said, "Are there any more boys around here going to try to win ponies?" But it didn't make any difference, they couldn't discourage us. "Never say fail," was our motto.

Well, our own little "Rob Roy" arrived here O. K. Tuesday afternoon at five o'clock. I was so happy and tickled I ran all the way to the field where papa was plowing corn to tell him and to have him help me get him home from the depot. It looked like rain and it didn't take us long to get there as papa hooked up the mules to the wagon and drove down.

When we got there the beautiful buggy and harness were there, too. We loaded them all on the wagon and started home with our big load.

Railroad Crossing (rc)

"Rob Roy" and "Babe" Doing Tricks

148

BY HAROLD KUTZLER, McCOOK CO., SOUTH DAKOTA

Roy Brown, who won "Babe" a couple of years ago from the Webb Publishing Company, is our neighbor. Roy went along to the station with us. There were so many people around "Rob Roy" and I was so excited, I thought I never would get him out home.

Well, we got him home finally and took him out of the crate. He was so tickled to get out that he would roll, then buck and kick and then roll some more. I took him in his little barn that we had all built and ready waiting for him. I even had hay in the manger and oats in the box. After we got "Rob Roy" cared for, we went to setting up the buggy and putting the harness together already for morning. Then I had supper and went to bed so happy and tired.

When morning came I woke up and thought I had been dreaming. I got up and went out to the barn and sure enough there was my little pony.

He looked up at me as if to say, "Good Morning." I went in and kissed his soft warm little nose, got him his quart of oats and a little hay and went for my breakfast. After we had our breakfast we were off for a ride.

"Rob Roy" is coal black and as cute and pretty as he can be. He will eat crackers, ice cream, cake, apples, bananas and many other things. He chased Roy Brown and me up on the porch after our cookies the other day and if he had not been tied, he would have been up there, too. We gave him his, but that wouldn't do, he wanted ours, too. He comes right in the house every time he gets a chance and if the table is set, goes right for the sugar bowl.

"Rob Roy" is so gentle he will do anything we want him to. I can ride and drive him anywhere. He is so proud and not one bit lazy.

continued on page 151

"Rob Roy" With His "Beautiful Buggy and Harness"

149

*O*ur papa and mamma take quite a few papers and we like to read them, and often saw advertisements in them of ponies being given away. We always wanted to try to get one but mama said she thought we couldn't get enough anyway, but we teased her so much, at last she said we could try, if papa would consent, thinking that if we tried and got left, we would be satisfied and not tease her any more.

Nearly every one tried to discourage us, saying we would probably get a sawhorse or else nothing. Even papa said to the last day we wouldn't get thirty cents. But we kept right on and had mamma on our side and she spoke a good word for us when she could.

We were so tickled when we got word that we had won a pony that we just jumped and shouted. "Mickey" was quite a while coming, owing to various delays and when he finally got to Brandon, we couldn't get him home for two days as it had rained so much the rivers were overflowed and the water was even over the bridges. The third day papa managed to get him home by going way around. My! We were tickled to see him.

"Mickey" soon got so he would follow us around everywhere. He is about 43 inches high and weighed 245 pounds when he came, but is sleek and fat now so we think he weighs more than 300 pounds now.

My sister Lucy rode "Mickey" after the mail several times so one day I thought I would ride him, as our mail box is nearly a mile from home,

***Homeward Bound* (rh)**

but "Mickey" dumped me off. He was only having fun with me, though, because I can ride him anywhere now.

"Mickey" isn't afraid of autos and he likes corn and oats better than sugar.

We did not get a buggy so couldn't drive our pony till just lately. One rainy day papa and the hired man made a little cart and fixed some straps for a harness. What fun we did have when they hitched him up. Papa went to get on the seat first and he slipped right off backwards in

Whose Turn First?

the mud. Then the hired man got on and drove around some and stopped in the yard a while. Then he thought he would start out again but "Mickey" wanted to go in the barn and the man pulled on the line so suddenly he tipped right over backwards in the mud with the cart and pony on top of him. How we all did laugh! Nobody got hurt.

One man offered $75.00 for our pony but we wouldn't sell him. Everybody thinks he is so cute.

The first time we drove him to school the children all thought he was fine. One day the harness broke and he got away from us and ran right home into the barn and broke our cart, so we have to walk to school till we get another rig. Thanks many times for dear little "Mickey."

OUR OWN LITTLE "ROB ROY"
continued from page 149

He will stand upon a box or chair. "Rob Roy" weighs 240 pounds and can pull Roy and Ruth Brown, my little sister and myself anywhere at a merry clip. Sometimes I take mamma and my little sister with me, but it doesn't make one bit of difference; he goes right along. He will look around as if to say, "All pile on" and does not make one bit of fuss. I have a little brown house dog named "Billy" and he goes with us and sometimes "Rob Roy" thinks we are running races with "Billy." "Billy" was my only pet before my pony arrived.

I am never going to sell my dear little pony at any price. I can say that I love The Farmer and can't thank the Webb Publishing Company enough for my little pony and his beautiful outfit.

Mamma went to town one day to do a little shopping so she sent me with my little brother over to grandma's until she came back. While Brother and I were playing it began to rain so Grandma made us come in the house and play. She gave us a lot of paper to write on and play school with. She also gave us some books and magazines to look at. In looking through the magazines, I found one called The Farmer's Wife, and taking it by the name, I looked through it, thinking I might find something that would help papa in his garden work. I did too, but when I looked a little farther, I saw a dear little Shetland Pony. This made me forget everything else, as I have wanted papa to buy me one for such a long time. I showed the pony to Grandma and asked her if I could cut it out, as I was going to ask papa if he would buy me one. Grandma said I could cut it out, so I did.

It did not stop raining all that day so I had to stay at Grandma's until mamma came after me and I was getting restless waiting for her, because I could not wait until I showed it to mamma and papa. At last mamma came and we went home; not long after papa came home from his work. Before he even had time to kiss me, I told him I wanted a pony. He laughed at me at first when I asked him and tried to discourage me, but I still bothered him, till he finally consented to let me write to The Farmer's Wife to find out how I could get a Shetland Pony free. Finding out how easy it was to get one, I joined the Pony Club for

Rain or Shine (rs)

luck; not expecting in the least to get a pony, as everybody that I would mention it to said I was only wasting time as The Webb Publishing Company could never afford to give me a pony for nothing. Some people would say, "Don't bother with it, John, they will send you one cut out of paper." I began to get discouraged myself a little then, but I wanted a pony and I knew the only way I would get one was to do my best and try to win. As papa said, "Nothing tried, nothing gained" and this proved true with me. I had nothing to lose so started out one day to get subscriptions. I got a few and when papa saw I was in earnest, he started out and mamma, too, to help me. Before long, we were all getting subscribers easy. The time went by so fast that it did not seem any time till the last day came. Then came the anxious moments. Day after day I would sit at the station watching the freight cars being unloaded to see if I had won my pony, but none came for over a week and I was just about giving up hopes for winning when, one day while I was playing outside, the mail man came along and called to me, "John, here is a letter for you." You should have seen my face brighten up. I was all smiles when I read it. It said, Dear John, you have won your pony and it will be shipped in a few days." So it did come a couple of days after.

continued on next page

"Robin"
Fenton Brannon, Meade Co., Kansas

"Robin" is the cutest pony you ever did see. The first night he was here, papa left the barn window open and he got out and ran away and when papa brought him home he looked so funny. You ought to have seen him; he looked like a little boy that had run off and his father had given him a spanking.

My brother just over a year old runs out and tries to ride him. We have the most fun with him. When he came the girls and boys all came to see him. "Robin" will shake hands with us. I thank the Webb Publishing Company.

continued

"Busy" is very well satisfied with his new home and we do everything we can to make him stay happy and to make him comfortable. Papa had a very nice stable built for "Busy" and he enjoys his bed very much after eating in the fields all day. I have had a good many saddle-back rides with "Busy" and he is as gentle as a little lamb. We have a governess cart so we take "Busy" out often and he looks just too cute for anything in his new set of harness and walks very proud. I just wish you could see him, how fine he looks and how he makes his ears stick up straight when he hears the folks compliment-ing him as we drive all along the road. "Busy" does not seem to have gotten any larger since we have had him, but he has gotten much fatter. "Busy" gets up every morning with papa as he knows it is time for his raw egg and oats. After he gets through his breakfast, we drive papa to the train and in the evening we go after him. "Busy" knows the time as well as I do, for when it is time he is standing right in the carriage shed waiting to be hitched up.

"Busy" can do all kinds of tricks. He can tell his own age; play that he is dead; stand with his front feet on a chair, and several other things. "Busy" was in the Fireman's Parade on the Fourth of July and he did splendid. I was rid-ing him saddle back and we were right behind the band, which pleased "Busy" very much. He dearly loves music and he was looked at and

Lucky Star (ls)

praised more than anything else in the parade. Everybody thought "Busy" would be scared or get balky when the band started, but he marched along as proud as the firemen. You can see how gentle he was and what a short time it took him to learn.

"Busy" feels the proudest when he is pulling a heavy load. He likes to go to picnics, because the girls and boys dearly love him and they give him fruit, candy, cakes, lump sugar, peanuts, popcorn or whatever they have. He is always at the table first and never leaves it until there is no more to eat. "Busy" helps papa to cultivate his garden, get in the hay, cut the lawn and does all the shopping for grandma and mamma.

I don't know how any little boy or girl can be without a pony, especially when they are so easy

"Hauling Hay for Papa"

to get from The Farmer's Wife. I was offered two hundred dollars for my pony "Busy," one Sunday morning by our newspaper man. He says he has been trying so long to get one for his little girls, and I told him he could not buy "Busy" for a thousand. If you want to win a pony, it is very easy as the Webb Publishing Company will certainly treat you fair and see that you get one before they let you be disappointed. I love "Busy" so much that I'm getting poetic—here's a sample:

I won my dear old "Busy,"
 In a very busy way;
Selling monthly papers for
The Farmer's Wife one day.

I am now going to write you my story, how it happened that I entered your Pony Club. Some years ago I answered your ad in some farm paper that you were going to give away a pony, but did not enter the Club at that time because everybody said it was no use of trying for I would not stand one speck of a show of winning. But I have been watching your pony publication ever since and have been teasing my folks to enter until they finally gave in and let me enter. I do not think they ever thought of my winning when I first entered, but when they saw what luck I was having on the start, they began to get interested, too, so they began to encourage me the best they could. My brother Oscar was out several days and sister Hannah was out with me most of the time and believe me, Mr. Editor, neither I nor my folks are sorry now for what we have done and if I should bring out in addition feelings within my heart, I certainly would kiss you for all you have done for me for I certainly have the cutest little pony of the whole Club and he is the pet of the whole family. Yes, of the whole neighborhood, too, for that matter, for children for miles around have come here to admire "Scrappy" and so smart is he that I think he understands every word I say to him and he will come to me whenever I call him.

Sugar Bowl (sb)

"I Have the Cutest Pony of the Whole Club"

156

He is very fond of apples, sugar, watermelon and many other things and just loves to drink milk, too. One real hot day this summer we set the table under some trees near the house and when we all were seated at the table up came "Scrappy" and wanted a place at the table, too, just as if he were one of the family. Of course, I gave him a lump of sugar and then had to turn him away, but I am sure his feelings were hurt for he went away from the table and went west of the grove and stayed away all afternoon as if he were going to show us that if he were not welcome to associate with us he would not bother us any more but I think he has forgotten it all by now, for he is himself again.

"Praising My Pony All the Day Long"

We were threshing our wheat the other day and I was a little afraid that "Scrappy" would get frightened and run into something and hurt himself but when the big steam engine came he was not any more afraid of that than of one of his best chums and when the engine blew its whistle, he just pricked up his ears and looked at it as cool and quiet as the man that was running it. He is a courageous little thing and not afraid of anything, and he is very playful. He plays with the colts and seems to be very much delighted in playing with the calves in the yard, too.

We went to visit a neighbor the other day and of course the rest of the family went in an auto, but you can bet that I did not go with them in that kind of a rig. I just got my pony and saddle and bridle and I think I attracted more attention with my rig than they did with theirs.

Well, I must now close my story, but before I close I will say to all boys and girls that they can't imagine what fun and pleasure they can have with a pony before they get one. I wish all boys and girls that have won a pony and all those that will win hereafter, all joy and happiness that life can possibly bring and especially you, Editor, for your good work in making boys and girls happy by giving them Shetland Ponies. And then one thing more: I wish to say to those that were in the Pony Club with me and all other Pony winners that I would like to exchange pictures and postal cards with all of you. It seems to me as if we all belonged to the same family.

So this is my story and this is my song, Praising my pony all the day long.

157

Darling "Dimple"

I want to thank the Webb Publishing Company for sending me such a dandy pony and outfit. I have only had "Dimple" a few months but I love him so that no amount of money could buy him. He is so gentle and kind that all of my little friends and I can play with him just as though he were a big dog. My folks are so glad that I own "Dimple" because I am out of doors playing with him so much I am keeping strong and healthy.

When I first started to take subscriptions lots of people said I couldn't get enough in so small a place and if I did that I would probably get a rocking horse as a prize, but I didn't mind them and went right on. I showed them a copy of "Lucky Pony Winners" and then they agreed that I would get a real Shetland pony. Everyone seemed to think the paper was fine, so the work wasn't hard after all.

When "Dimple" first came he had long shaggy hair and didn't look so cute, but in the Spring my brother clipped him and now his hair is smooth and fine. We feed him lots of oats and green grass and he is getting so fat that we have to drive him a lot to keep

Sheep Fold (sf)

Ida and "Dimple"

158

him in good condition. He certainly is strong and can pull a crowd of us along as fast as any horse and it is nothing at all for him to travel sixteen miles a day.

"Dimple" likes bread, apples, candy and anything sweet and he is so affectionate that I must tell you about it. If I tell him to kiss me, he will and he seems to like to kiss me.

Nearly every day "Dimple" goes out in the pasture and plays around with our sheep. It certainly is funny to see him chase them around, shaking his head and nipping at them, but he knows he shouldn't hurt them because just as soon as they get frightened, he stops and goes off and lets them rest.

I have so many good times with my pony and buggy that I can hardly tell you about them. If only every boy and girl owned a pony like "Dimple," they would be very happy and I believe any one can get a pony from the Webb Publishing Company, if he is willing to do a little work for them. They always do exactly as they say and you can always feel sure that you will get your pony if you are entitled to it.

I certainly am glad that I sent my name to the Pony Editor and hope he will make lots of other children as happy as he made me by giving them a darling little pony like "Dimple."

"He Is So Gentle and Kind"

I want to tell other little boys and girls how I won my pony. When I started to get subscriptions I had great hopes of getting one of the ponies, but a few weeks after I entered the contest I had to give up school on account of my health, so just as I ought to have been getting subscriptions I couldn't. I was pretty well discouraged and would have given it up if I had not received such encouraging letters from the Pony Editor.

My health improved in a short time but I had only a few weeks left in which to get subscriptions. I began again but could not go far from home to get them as I had but little time to spare. We live near a small town in which but few people own land; I only secured a few there and at the last we were so anxious that we worked hard and got most of the subscriptions in a short time.

When I received a letter from the Pony Club telling me I had not won a pony I said I would try to win a special pony because I knew they would treat me fairly. I wrote and asked them about their "Special Pony Contest" and they sent me instructions how to do it and how they would

Star of Hope (sh)

Feeding "Sugar, Plums and Honey"

give me a year to get subscriptions. I entered that and my pony "Bruce" came in about three weeks.

When I knew he was coming I could hardly wait to get him and I thought those three weeks were the longest ones I ever lived. One morning my brother and I were away from home and while we were gone the pony came to the station. The expressman telephoned mamma that "Bruce" had arrived.

When we came home mamma told us to eat our dinner in a hurry as we had some hard work to do. We wondered what it was and asked two or three times. When she told us we fairly jumped up and down.

We only had "Bruce" two days when my brother was seriously hurt when in town and we could not bring him home for two weeks. He was very anxious to see "Bruce" and wanted to see him so much that we led him right into the house and into brother's room. "Bruce" put his little nose down to the bed and seemed to know something was wrong. When we brought him out on the porch we took a picture of him as you see above my story.

We are very happy with "Bruce" and cannot get along without him.

"Out for a Jolly Good Time"

I am so glad I joined The Farmer's Wife Pony Club, for I got one of the prettiest and sweetest little spotted ponies you ever saw. But while I was working to win him I would get awfully discouraged sometimes as some people would refuse to take my paper and say, "You know you can't get enough subscribers to get a pony as there are so many boys and girls in larger towns who are working for them," but mother would tell me not to give up, so I got some of my friends to help me and I got one.

Floral Bouquet (sp)

His name is "Wuzzy" and when I call him he just comes running. We keep him out in the front yard most all the time and last spring mother wanted some flowers in the yard and he didn't bother them at all till they began to bloom and we commenced picking them to make bouquets. Then he would go and look at them and bite the blossoms off, but mother didn't scold much for she knew he just thought they were pretty and he looked so cute and full of mischief when he would bite them off.

My little brother loves "Wuzzy" so. I was away on a visit ten weeks this summer and my little brother attended to him

"'Wuzzy' Loves to Have Us Play with Him"

while I was gone. He rode after the mail for mother. He said when "Wuzzy" wanted water he would come right up the steps and into the house to get himself some water. My brother rode him a mile last Sunday to the station by himself.

One of "Wuzzy's" Tricks

I never will forget the night my little "Wuzzy" came. My little brother and I had gone to bed and mother came and called us and told us our little pony had come. We got up and dressed and the depot agent went with us to get him. He was the gladest little thing to get out of his crate and get to his new home. The little boys and girls came to see him next morning as soon as they heard he had come, and they would say, "I didn't think you would get a pony sure enough." They love to play with him. They will hug and kiss him and Oh! he is so pretty and sweet. I expect he gets lonesome when we are at school for he loves for us to play with him.

I had a letter from a little girl in Jackson, Tenn., asking me to tell her about my little pony. Said she heard I got one and she wanted to join the Pony Club and if she has joined I hope to see her name with the lucky ones in the next contest.

I must close but would love to write lots more about our dear little pony "Wuzzy."

'*Twas on a* cold night in February when we were sitting around the fire-side, Father and Mother reading and Sister amusing herself with a game, that I grew tired of looking at the pictures in the fire and became restless. Mother told me to go to bed, but I objected as I was not sleepy. Father asked me to please find something to do and get quiet so he could read with some satisfaction. Going over to the machine, on which a stack of papers were lying, I looked for a story to read. Very soon I found something quite interesting to a boy. It was the picture of a pony and cart on the back of The Progressive Farmer. Taking the paper with me, I went back to my chair to read about the pony, but I was quiet only a few minutes, for I soon learned that the Webb Publishing Company was giving ponies to girls and boys who would do a little work for them, and the thought that I might be one of the lucky ones filled me with such joy that Father was unable to read because of my questions until after I had crawled into bed to think, and think, and think of my pony and then to dream of him.

The next morning my letter to the Company started on its journey and in a few days a letter came from them telling me the kind of work to do. I was delighted to learn that it was such pleasant work as getting subscriptions for The Farmer's Wife and began at once. I got thirty-two subscriptions the first day, which showed me I could do the work and encouraged me to go ahead with it.

Seminole Square (ss)

Some people tried to discourage me, saying, "You are wasting your time for that Company will not give you a pony," and many other things to make me doubt the fairness of the Pony Club. But I continued to dream of my pony and to work to get it, believing that I would surely win and the Company would treat me right. I soon learned from boys and girls who had worked for ponies that I would get the pony if I won it as the Company was thoroughly reliable. This encouraged me to work still harder.

About a week after the contest closed, a letter came saying I had won "White Sox" and he would be shipped to me the last of the week. How happy I was! My dream had come true. In a few days, I received a beautiful bridle and saddle. These caused me to watch more anxiously for my pony and cart. I met each train and when I would learn that no pony was "on board" it seemed that I could not wait until the next train came. Finally on Tuesday night I met the local train and, much to my grief, no pony came.

The fast train—the beautiful Seminole Limited from Chicago to Jacksonville, Florida—was an hour late, so I came to supper and went back to the station at eight o'clock. When the long row of lighted windows of the Seminole stopped, I stepped up to the baggage coach and the first thing I saw was "White Sox." I really believe that was the happiest moment of my life. I could scarcely wait for him to be taken from the car.

continued on next page

Crayton and Sister Dressed Up for a Ride

continued

My home is in a small town, so when the neighbors heard us coming with the pony, all of them—large and small—came out to see him. The children wanted to ride him, but as it was late and he was hungry, I took him over to the lot where his supper was waiting.

He was so tired from the long trip, and of being fastened up in such a close place that he was glad to have us take him out. He seemed to like me from the first because I helped set him free from such a prison, and we have grown to be closer and closer friends each day.

It seemed almost too good to be true that I had a real live pony, but he is surely mine, and I shall now tell of the great pleasure he has been to me, Sister and my friends. Five little cousins and several friends were introduced to him the night he came, each gave him a welcoming pat on the nose, and now all of them are close friends of his.

He likes for us to play ball with him. We bound the ball on the ground near him and he catches it with his mouth. One day we were playing with watermelon rinds—having a rind battle—and when we

Alabama (al)

A Watermelon Feast

would "chunk" a rind at him he would catch it. It pleases him much to give him fruit, sugar or cake. When we call him he comes running to see what good we have for him. We make him "say please," which he does by pawing his foot. He likes sugar very much. Often he goes into Father's store and eats sugar from the floor around the sugar barrels. One day while I was away on a visit to my aunt, he went in the back of the store and walked up to the desk as though he would write me a letter telling me how he missed me and asking me to come home.

Now, don't you think he is quite an interesting pony, and are you surprised that my friends and I, who have so much fun with him, would not part with him for anything? I feel that I cannot thank the Webb Publishing Company enough for him. Every little boy and girl should have a pony. There is nothing that equals one as a play-fellow, and anyone who is willing to do a little work for the Webb Publishing Company can get one of his very own.

TO MY PONY "SLICK"
JOSEPH KOTTUM, RENVILLE CO., MINNESOTA

I am a boy just ten years old,
And a bad one at that, so I'm told.
I joined the Pony Club early last spring,
And won a very beautiful thing.

Buggy, harness, saddle and horse,
A Shetland Pony I mean, of course.
His color is brown, his name is "Slick,"
He is kind and gentle, active and quick.

My pony can neither be traded nor sold,
For to me he is worth his weight in gold.
He weighs not much, just three hundred pounds,
For a real live pony how little it sounds.

When tired of work and tired of play,
I hitch up "Slick" and drive away.
I go to neighbors, friends and town,
In fact I drive him all around.

When people stop me on the street
And ask where I got my outfit so neat,
I tell them the Pony Man gave him to me,
For getting a few subscriptions, you see.

Good luck to the Company and thanks to you all,
Who subscribed for the paper, both large and small.
The Webb Publishing Company I'll never forget,
For sending me such a beautiful pet.

*Y*es, *"Hero" is* my pony's name and he is a real hero, too. Of course, everyone who has a Shetland pony likes him, but I think my pony is the best and no other pony could be so dear to me as my little "Hero."

He is mostly black and single white hairs are spread here and there among the black and the upper part of his tail is clear white and both hinds legs are white.

I always liked horses, and I have gone horseback riding on one of my father's horses since I was about seven years old, but when I saw the pictures of the cute Shetland ponies in papers I wished and wished that I could get one—one that I could have for my own. Then I happened to see that The Webb Publishing Co. was going to give away a Shetland pony as first prize in a contest and I thought I would try to win the pony. I tried my best, but did not win the pony that time. Oh, I tell you I felt sorry when I heard that I didn't win the pony. I got a nice prize but it wasn't the long wished for pony.

The next year I had a letter from the company and they asked me if I wanted to try once more. Then they were going to give away "Hero." I thought I must try again—there must be a better chance now. But my mother said: "Don't bother with that, you can't win a pony anyhow; that's too hard a contest for a little girl." I begged and begged and after a while I got leave to try again.

I started out right away. As often as I could have one of my father's horses I hustled away horseback.

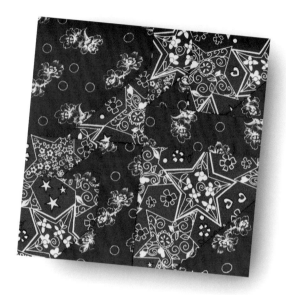

Telephone (te)

I tried to do my best and get as many subscribers as I could and I think it wasn't so hard after all to win my pony. But I will never forget how I felt when I got the letter that told me I had won "Hero." I could hardly believe it was true. The day the pony came to our nearest town, they telephoned us from the depot and told us that the pony was there.

It was late in the afternoon, but father went to town to get the pony home anyhow. It was no wonder that my brother and I couldn't go to sleep that evening before father came home with the pony. It was very late, but the moon shone bright so we couldn't help playing a little while with "Hero." When we went to bed I whispered to my brother: "If you should happen to wake up before I do tomorrow morning, please call me so we can be outside with 'Hero' a long while before we go to school. If I wake up first I'll call you." How early we went out the next morning, I don't know what time it was, but we had been outside a long while when father and mother got up at five o'clock.

We were very tired in school that day and I couldn't study because my thoughts went to my pony.

continued on next page

Don't These Boys Wish They Owned "Hero?"

169

continued

It would be too long a story if I should tell you of all the fun and use we have had of the pony, but I'll tell you a few cute things that will show you how smart my cute little "Hero" is.

We always go out the back door when we go to the barn, or to feed the chickens and we always have something with us for "Hero," who has his liberty to go where he wants to in the whole yard. We give him sugar and bread, cake, fruits and scraps from the table.

When he noticed that we always went out the back door with food for him he always came to that door, placing his front feet on the third step by the side of the door and stood there knocking and many times he has fooled us. We sometimes think it is somebody on two feet who wants to see us, but when we open the door there stands little "Hero" knocking, and when he sees us he begs with his voice as you know horses do, and he never begged in vain, I tell you.

A little girl about 3 years old visited us one time. She liked to give "Hero" something to eat, but once she sat on the porch steps eating a piece of cake, that she wanted herself. "Hero" likes cake, too, and he walked right to the little girl and put his nose in her hands and took the cake. "Mind your own business," said the little girl, who had a very quick tongue, and had heard her parents say these words to her, but "Hero" swallowed the cake and walked on.

Morning Star (ms)

If it happens that we don't have anything to give "Hero" when we come out he will put his nose into our hands and stand looking at us in wonder.

He can jump upon the porch and down just as he pleases. If we play in the yard he follows us; if we run, he runs after us. All the children in the neighborhood like "Hero" and often

170

come to our place and we have a good time play-ing with him.

When we are out driving him we often meet automobiles and the noisy motorcycles that have scared so many horses, but my brave little "Hero" knows better than to get scared. I never saw a thing that could frighten him, so I think he is a sure enough little hero.

We Have Good Times Playing With "Hero"

*N*ow *I am* going to tell you all what fine times I have with my dear little pony "Tatters." I won him last May. When I told my friends that I was going to try to get a pony by getting subscribers for The Farmer they laughed at me but I knew the Webb Publishing Company did just as they said they would so I just let them laugh and I worked all the harder.

We lived at Foreston, Minnesota when I won my pony and the 4th of August we started to drive through to where we are now at Bear River, Minn. It was nearly three hundred miles the way we came. Papa got me a little cart and harness for my pony so that I could drive him myself on the road here and I just wish you could have seen him. He would haul when we would come to big hills and bad roads and he was just as fast as he could be all the way and some days we would go 30 or 35 miles in one day and he wouldn't be as tired as the big horses were. And when we would go through a town there would be a dozen or more boys and girls that would follow us way out of town and they would all have to know where I got such a nice little pony. When we would camp at night we would camp near some town or farm house so that we could get water and

Trail of the Covered Wagon (tr)

"We Drove Nearly 300 Miles"

there would be so many that would come down to our tent and the first thing they went to was my pony. I could have sold him every place we stopped but I would tell them that he wasn't for sale.

He can do a few tricks. He will shake hands and kiss me or will lie down and get up again with me on his back and will come to me when I call him, and if the door is open he will come right in the house and look all over for sugar. He likes apples, candy and bread. Oh! I think he is just the dearest playmate that there is, so good and kind. I like to put my little saddle on him and go for a ride. He will run so fast when I tell him to and he don't throw me off.

You would laugh if you could see him when my little brother goes for a ride. He will trot slow and easy so brother won't fall off as he is only four years old. We both ride some times but "Tatters" likes to take us one at a time the best. Guess he is afraid to hurt some of us when there is more than one on his back.

Well now, I think my letter is long enough, still I could talk about my pony for a week yet. I think he is so nice and I think the Webb Publishing Company are so good to give away such dear little playmates, as I am sure I would never have got a pony if it hadn't been for them so I thank them very much.

We're Off!

I want to tell every little boy and girl about "Ad," the darling "Special Pony" The Farmer's Wife Pony Club gave me. We have many good times together and I love to see him romp and play. I do wish you could be here today and see dear little "Ad" try to follow my mamma and papa off with "Daddy Boy," my papa's horse. "Dad" loves "Ad." I did not think "Dad" would make up with "Ad" as he is a very mean horse around children. He don't like children at all and since "Ad" came to our home, I think "Dad" has begun to like me and I want to tell you that no one could buy him from me for he is my dearest friend. I have no sisters or brothers and you know I am having a big time with "Ad."

I have been offered $200.00 for him but that will not buy him for he is a dear little pony. You can see by his pictures how sweet he is. He looks rough but after he sheds off his long hair I will get a better picture. I had so many try to discourage me but they can all see what the Pony Editor and the Webb Publishing Company is and they are the fairest people, my mamma and papa said, that they ever had any dealing with.

You all will never imagine how proud I am of "Ad." My pictures were taken

Virginia (va)

Aurelia, "Ad," Papa and "Daddy Boy"

174

in our back yard and I was only on dear little "Ad's" back long enough for my mamma to snap the picture. I am not going to ride him much now because he is rather young yet. I think he can pull a little cart better than he can ride me on his back so Grandpa is going to make me a little sulky for this winter, a light one.

I take him every day to my grandma's to eat grass. I wish you could see him eat. He loves oats. My mamma and I have lots of fun with "Ad." When she hangs her clothes out he goes up to the clothes basket and runs off with a piece of the clothes in his mouth. (And, my dear Pony Editor, if you ever do come to Norfolk, please don't forget you promised me in your letter if you would come to Norfolk that you would look me up. Please don't forget.)

Well, I guess I must close as I know some more anxious children are writing the Pony Editor

"How Proud I Am"

and want their letters read too, and published in "Lucky Pony Winners" and if I write such a long letter I will not give him a chance to read the other children's letters and I do not want to be selfish as I know they love their ponies as well as I love mine and I would love to write to all the children that have ponies and tell them how nice the Webb Publishing Company was to a little girl in Norfolk, Va. And I will be glad to write to any that care to write to me, for the Pony Editor is the dearest one on earth to make me so happy.

Love to all the Webb Publishing Company and may they have a successful year in 1915, and may the boys and girls work next year and win a prize like mine. Your little friends, Aurelia and "Ad."

My pony, "Hector," is a nice little brown pony, weighs three hundred and fifty pounds and is forty-six inches high. He is just as cute as he can be. I went to the station every day and finally when he did come on April 11th I was not there. But my papa telephoned that the pony was there. We nearly turned the house over for joy. The first Sunday we had him most everybody came to see him, and they all thought he was so nice.

I love little "Hector" and he loves me and he follows me everywhere. If I call him he will come falling over everything he meets, because he thinks he will get something to eat.

I race with my little brother Alfred on another pony but he is so slow I beat him every time. Oh, if you all could see me! But if other children work for The Farmer's Wife they will get a pony alright. I wish all little girls and boys could have such a pony as I have and have such a good time as I have. But if they all work for The Farmer's Wife they won't have to work all their lives, only a couple of months will do.

Verna Belle's Favorite (vb)

"Hector" and Baby Are Good Friends

I was going to get the cows one day with "Hector" and I found all mamma's geese and I brought them home so mamma could give them some cheese. You can see the geese in one of my pictures.

"Hector" rides on the automobile sometimes and that makes him feel like he is the biggest horse in the country, but when he is down again he sees that he is only a little Shetland Pony.

My dear little school friends wanted to ride my pony once and have their picture taken with him. See in one of the pictures how little "Hector" is climbing into baby Violet's cradle because he is getting some sugar. My little sister Violet loves "Hector" so if she sees him she cries that she wants to get on for a ride.

I was riding into the house one day to see what mamma was doing but she turned me out because the pony was chewing on some sugar. He is always climbing on the table looking for something to eat, but I won't give him anything because that isn't nice.

I am only eleven years old now, but if I am big and married sometime and far away from home then my sister Violet will have little "Hector" to enjoy all alone. But days will pass and years and he might get too old and certainly he will die some day and then she will bury him under a stone where the sun has never shone. But I don't like to think so far ahead.

I can't tell you how much I thank the Webb Publishing Co. for giving me such a smart little pony. I will always remember them as long as I live. I hope you will like the pictures.

"I Found All Mamma's Geese"

What "Larry" Means to Me

I have had the finest kind of times since I won my little pony "Larry" and I want to tell you some of the cute things he will do. Quite often my neighbor children come over then I take "Larry" and saddle him up and he gives each one of us a ride. Then we put "Larry" on the goat wagon and haul him around a while. He stands up there and looks all around and never moves when we pull him around. We then let "Larry" eat all the apples he can eat. He takes bites out of an apple just like a person and just the size of a person's bite.

I have two miles to go to school. I go to school in town. Every morning I saddle "Larry" up and he takes me to school. "Larry" had a three months' vacation and now he has to saddle to school again. My school just started last Tuesday and now "Larry" has to go every day again. When I come to school in the mornings, the girls and boys all ask me for a ride on the pony.

"Larry often eats sugar out of a saucer. Every time he wants sugar if there is a chair or a box outside he gets on it no matter if I am on his back or not. He will get on a chair or a box and beg for sugar; that is, he neighs for sugar. There isn't a

Village School House (vs)

"Larry" Ready for the Fourth of July Parade

178

store in town where he hasn't been in. He goes in the drug store and the druggist knows he wants ice cream and he bows enough to say, "Yes." He gives him a cone of ice cream and "Larry" will eat every bit of it and then looks for more. Then he will drink pop and root beer right of a glass in the drug store. Then the druggist gives him some gum and he will chew the gum and I am on his back all the time. Then I go in a grocery store he will eat sugar lumps right off the counter. The clerk will ask the pony if he wants a banana and he will bow enough to say, "yes." "Larry likes oranges and cookies. He will eat cake and bread. He will eat anything I eat.

Last year "Larry" and I went to our Fourth of July parade. Mother made "Larry" a nice fly net of red, white and blue bunting. It is four miles from my home to where they had their celebration.

Both Proud of the Picture

When I got to our town they all shouted, "Hurrah, hurrah, for the red, white and blue pony and boy." When I started from town to go down to the lake the automobiles that passed by me said, "Hurrah, hurrah, for the red, white and blue."

When I got down to the celebration I had to go across a bridge and someone took a picture and I did not know it till afterwards when she showed me the pictures. I made lots of money that day for going up and down the picnic grounds.

"Larry" is not scared of automobiles or motorcycles. The first time he met an automobile he made a face at it. The driver of the automobile laughed and said I had a great pony. "Larry" is not scared of anything and I hope I will never have to part with him.

I have wanted to write long before this to tell you all about my good times with "Clipper," and send you some pictures, but it was hard to get good pictures because "Clipper" seemed bashful and always turned the wrong way just in time to spoil them.

Just about a year ago I won "Clipper," and he traveled all the way from Minnesota to Massachusetts in a little crate. One of our neighbors brought him out here in his express wagon, and I just guess I was tickled to see him and know that he was a really truly Shetland pony that I could ride and drive. We got him out of his crate just as soon as we could, and fed and watered him and gave him a chance to lie down and rest. He was tired for two or three days, but after that the little saddle and bridle came and our fun began.

Western Star (ws)

"Clipper" never gets real frightened at anything. If he sees anything strange, all I have to do is to let him go up to it, sniff at it and look it all over and after that he is never afraid of it again. He isn't a bit afraid of automobiles. He quite often has one in the barn right side of his stall, and we have to tie him up so he can't reach out, for he seems to think the shiny mudguards are good to eat. If the motor is running he will walk right up to it and not even bother to look at it.

Playing Soldier

180

BY ADELAIDE J. STEVER, BRISTOL CO., MASSACHUSETTS

Then I first got "Clipper," I couldn't ride him very well and one night it was cold and he was in a hurry to get home to his supper. He started to gallop and I fell off. It didn't hurt but it scared me and I started to cry. "Clipper" had got quite a way down the road towards home, but when he heard me he stopped and listened and then turned around and trotted back. He came right up to me and stuck his little warm nose in my hand and kept putting up his front foot to shake hands with me, same as we taught him. He was trying so hard to tell me how sorry he was that I fell off, that it made me stop crying and begin to laugh. I got on and rode him home and he was as careful as could be all the rest of the way.

There is a little boy near here that I play with and we have lots of fun with "Clipper." Some times we play parade and I always carry the big flag and lead. When the drummer gets tired, why "Clipper" carries us both home and doesn't seem to mind the load a bit.

Adelaide and Russel Out for a Ride

I had a little Western saddle and a cowgirl suit for a birthday present and now we play Wild West a lot out in the big field. I lasso Russel or hold him up with my gun. "Clipper" seems to enjoy it as much as we do.

He is a splendid saddle pony. Daddy trained him to guide by the neck to single-foot, trot and canter, just like the big trained saddle horses, so now he is awfully easy to ride. I can guide him with the reins in one hand and he learned it all so easy that Daddy said there was no work at all in training him.

Sometimes, when my father and mother go on the big horses I go with them and "Clipper" keeps up with them as easy as anything.

He is such fun and such a nice pet that I don't see why all the boys and girls don't work and get subscriptions and get one like him. I can't thank The Farmer's Wife enough for making it possible for me to have such a dear little pony.

*W*onder whether any little boy or girl has had the experiences with their pony that I have had. I got terribly excited one day when I saw the pictures of little boys and their ponies in The Farmer's Wife and so I called, "Papa come here quick. See the nice little horses. Oh, how I wish I had one." Well, papa scratched his head and read all about the ponies and then said, "Well Bub, maybe we can win one." I tell you I clapped my hands for joy and shouted to mama, "Just think, mama, I think I can win a nice little pony." I worked a good long time for subscribers but never felt I had worked too hard when several weeks afterward I heard that my pony had been shipped. Long before it was even time for my pony to arrive, my friends and I used to run to the station but always with the same result—no pony—until one fine morning when, lo and behold, a real live pony was carried out of the baggage car and on the crate was written, "For Durrell V. Moyer, Macungie, Pa."

Well, I was happy and yet not happy. The little pony looked more like a bear with his long shaggy locks and long mane. Then, too, he was tired and wouldn't let me touch him. But papa knew that poor little

Young Man's Fancy (ym)

"And Now I Have Dandy Rides"

182

"Toodles" needed rest and something to eat, so we took him home and put him in the little stall we had built for him. In a few days "Toodles" seemed to feel better and he let me feed him, and pat him, and love him and today there isn't a sign

A Small Rough Rider

of any long hair and he's just the sweetest little pet I have ever had. I now have a nice little harness and wagon for him and I have dandy rides.

One night I had a terrible time. It grew dark suddenly and a storm came up, making the night all the more fearsome with its flashes of lightning and thunder that roared like a cannon. I only thought of my pony and how lonesome he must be with no papa or mama near him to take care of him. When it stopped raining I ran to the window to see whether all was safe in the barns. Then, horrors! What do you think I saw? Why a man with a lantern trying to unlock the door of my pony stall. I tried to scream so as to scare the burglar off but what more did he do but force the door open and lead "Toodles" out. I cried and cried until I heard mama say, "Come boy, it's time to get up now." Then I saw it was broad day light and my experiences only a dream. Was I glad to see my pony again? You bet I was. I have only the warmest spot in my heart for The Farmer's Wife which helped me to win my pony.

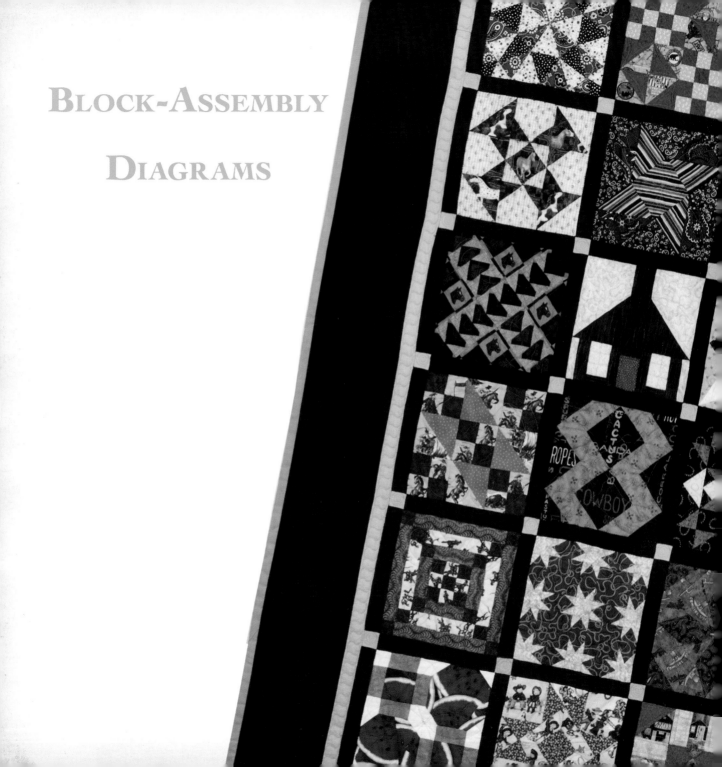

BLOCK-ASSEMBLY

DIAGRAMS

Block Assembly

Assemble the block according to the spaces between the pieces. Begin with the narrowest spaces. If no spaces are shown, the pieces can be assembled in any order.

ab 1
Cut 4.

ab 2   ab 2   ab 2R
Cut 4. Cut 4.   Cut 8.

ab 3
Cut 1.

ab 4
Cut 4.

Line
Diagram

Block Assembly

Assemble the block according to the spaces between the pieces. Begin with the narrowest spaces. If no spaces are shown, the pieces can be assembled in any order.

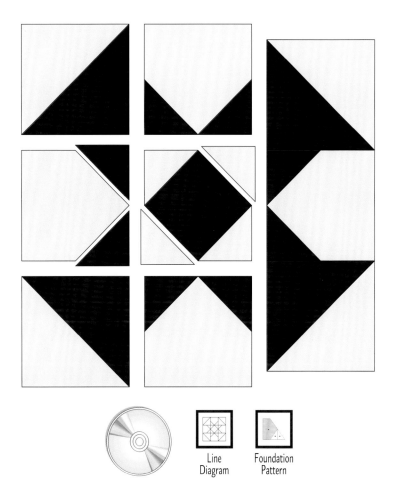

ad 1
Cut 4.

ad 1
Cut 8.

ad 2
Cut 1.

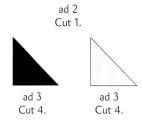

ad 3
Cut 4.

ad 3
Cut 4.

ad 4
Cut 4.

Line Diagram

Foundation Pattern

Block Assembly

Assemble the block according to the spaces between the pieces. Begin with the narrowest spaces. If no spaces are shown, the pieces can be assembled in any order.

al 1
Cut 4.

al 2
Cut 17

al 2
Cut 4.

al 3
Cut 4.

al 4
Cut 4.

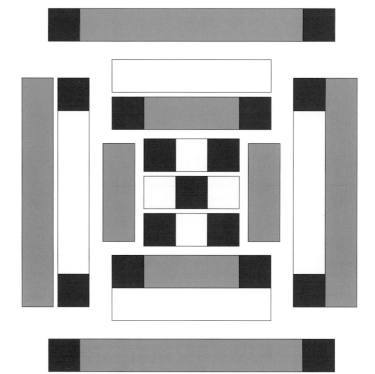

Line Diagram

Foundation Pattern

188

Block Assembly

Assemble the block according to the spaces between the pieces. Begin with the narrowest spaces. If no spaces are shown, the pieces can be assembled in any order.

See page 278 for a numbered assembly diagram.

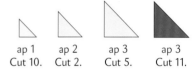

ap 1
Cut 10.

ap 2
Cut 2.

ap 3
Cut 5.

ap 3
Cut 11.

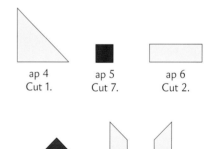

ap 4
Cut 1.

ap 5
Cut 7.

ap 6
Cut 2.

ap 7
Cut 1.

ap 8
Cut 1.

ap 8R
Cut 1.

Line
Diagram

Foundation
Pattern

Rotary
Cutting

189

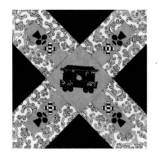

Block Assembly

Assemble the block according to the spaces between the pieces. Begin with the narrowest spaces. If no spaces are shown, the pieces can be assembled in any order.

at 1
Cut 4.

at 2
Cut 4.

at 2
Cut 8.

at 3
Cut 4.

at 4
Cut 1.

Line
Diagram

Foundation
Pattern

Rotary
Cutting

Block Assembly

Assemble the block according to the spaces between the pieces. Begin with the narrowest spaces. If no spaces are shown, the pieces can be assembled in any order.

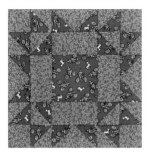

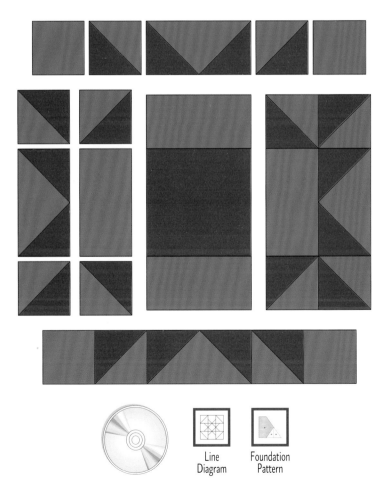

az 1
Cut 4.

az 2
Cut 20.

az 2
Cut 12.

az 3
Cut 4.

az 4
Cut 1.

az 5
Cut 4.

Line Diagram

Foundation Pattern

ba 1
Cut 4.

ba 2
Cut 4.

ba 3
Cut 2.

ba 4
Cut 4.

ba 5
Cut 1.

ba 6
Cut 2.

ba 7
Cut 1.

ba 8
Cut 4.

ba 9
Cut 2.

ba 10
Cut 2.

ba 11
Cut 1.

ba 11R
Cut 1.

Block Assembly

Assemble the block according to the spaces between the pieces. Begin with the narrowest spaces. If no spaces are shown, the pieces can be assembled in any order.

See page 278 for a numbered assembly diagram.

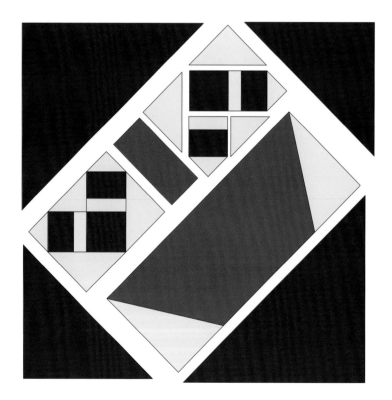

Line
Diagram

Foundation
Pattern

Rotary
Cutting

BETTY'S DELIGHT (bd)

Block Assembly

Assemble the block according to the spaces between the pieces. Begin with the narrowest spaces. If no spaces are shown, the pieces can be assembled in any order.

bd 1
Cut 4.

bd 1
Cut 4.

bd 2
Cut 4.

bd 2R
Cut 4.

bd 2
Cut 4.

bd 2R
Cut 4.

bd 3
Cut 4.

bd 3
Cut 4.

Line
Diagram

Foundation
Pattern

Rotary
Cutting

193

Block Assembly

Assemble the block according to the spaces between the pieces. Begin with the narrowest spaces. If no spaces are shown, the pieces can be assembled in any order.

be 1
Cut 4.

be 2
Cut 8.

be 3
Cut 16.

be 4
Cut 8.

be 5
Cut 8.

be 5
Cut 4.

be 6
Cut 1.

Line
Diagram

Foundation
Pattern

194

BEST FRIEND (bf)

Block Assembly

Assemble the block according to the spaces between the pieces. Begin with the narrowest spaces. If no spaces are shown, the pieces can be assembled in any order.

bf 1
Cut 16 .

bf 1
Cut 16.

bf 2
Cut 12.

bf 2
Cut 8.

bf 3
Cut 1.

bf 4
Cut 4.

Line
Diagram

Foundation
Pattern

Rotary
Cutting

195

Broken Heart (bh)

bh 1
Cut 12.

bh 2R
Cut 4.

bh 2
Cut 4.

bh 3
Cut 4.

bh 4
Cut 4.

bh 5
Cut 24.

bh 6
Cut 1.

bh 7
Cut 4.

Block Assembly

Assemble the block according to the spaces between the pieces. Begin with the narrowest spaces. If no spaces are shown, the pieces can be assembled in any order.

See page 278 for a numbered assembly diagram.

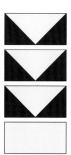

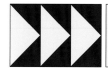

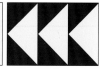

Line
Diagram

Foundation
Pattern

Block Assembly

Assemble the block according to the spaces between the pieces. Begin with the narrowest spaces. If no spaces are shown, the pieces can be assembled in any order.

bp 1
Cut 4.

bp 2
Cut 8.

bp 3
Cut 1.

bp 4
Cut 4.

Line
Diagram

Foundation
Pattern

Block Assembly

Assemble the block according to the spaces between the pieces. Begin with the narrowest spaces. If no spaces are shown, the pieces can be assembled in any order.

br 1
Cut 1.

br 2
Cut 1.

br 2
Cut 2.

br 2
Cut 1.

Line
Diagram

198

Block Assembly

Assemble the block according to the spaces between the pieces. Begin with the narrowest spaces. If no spaces are shown, the pieces can be assembled in any order.

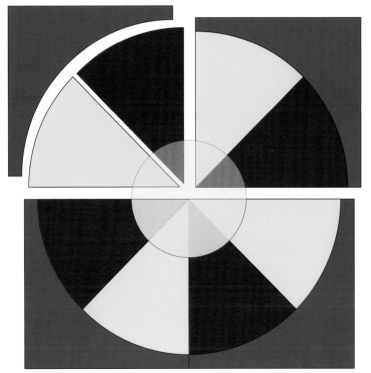

Line
Diagram

bv 1
Cut 1.

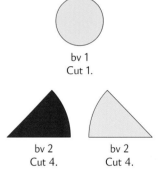

bv 2
Cut 4.

bv 2
Cut 4.

bv 3
Cut 4.

Assemble bv 2 and bv 3 pieces, then appliqué piece bv 1.

199

Block Assembly

Assemble the block according to the spaces between the pieces. Begin with the narrowest spaces. If no spaces are shown, the pieces can be assembled in any order.

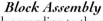

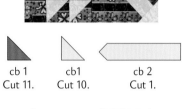

cb 1
Cut 11.

cb1
Cut 10.

cb 2
Cut 1.

cb 3
Cut 2.

cb 4
Cut 1.

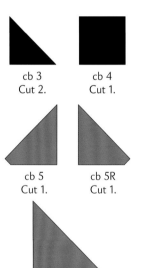

cb 5
Cut 1.

cb 5R
Cut 1.

cb 6
Cut 2.

Line
Diagram

Foundation
Pattern

Rotary
Cutting

COLT'S CORRAL (cc)

Block Assembly

Assemble the block according to the spaces between the pieces. Begin with the narrowest spaces. If no spaces are shown, the pieces can be assembled in any order.

cc 1
Cut 8.

 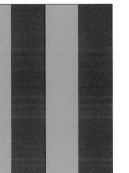

cc 1
Cut 12.

Line Diagram

Foundation Pattern

201

CHILDREN'S DELIGHT (cd)

Block Assembly

Assemble the block according to the spaces between the pieces. Begin with the narrowest spaces. If no spaces are shown, the pieces can be assembled in any order.

cd 1
Cut 5.

cd 2
Cut 4.

cd 3
Cut 2.

cd 4
Cut 1.

Line
Diagram

Foundation
Pattern

Block Assembly

Assemble the block according to the spaces between the pieces. Begin with the narrowest spaces. If no spaces are shown, the pieces can be assembled in any order.

See page 278 for a numbered assembly diagram.

cf 1
Cut 24.

cf 1
Cut 12.

cf 2
Cut 2.

cf 3
Cut 2.

cf 4
Cut 1.

cf 5
Cut 12.

cf 5
Cut 4.

cf 6
Cut 2.

cf 7
Cut 2.

cf 8
Cut 4.

Line Diagram

Foundation Pattern

203

Block Assembly

Assemble the block according to the spaces between the pieces. Begin with the narrowest spaces. If no spaces are shown, the pieces can be assembled in any order.

cl 1
Cut 4.

cl 2
Cut 8.

cl 2
Cut 9.

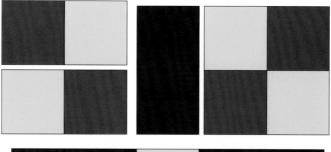

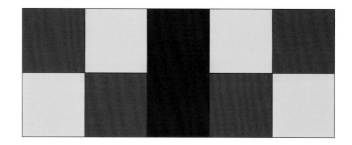

Line
Diagram

Foundation
Pattern

Block Assembly

Assemble the block according to the spaces between the pieces. Begin with the narrowest spaces. If no spaces are shown, the pieces can be assembled in any order.

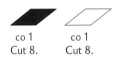

co 1
Cut 8.

co 1
Cut 8.

co 2
Cut 4.

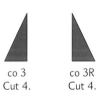

co 3
Cut 4.

co 3R
Cut 4.

Line
Diagram

Foundation
Pattern

205

CAT'S PAW (cp)

Block Assembly

Assemble the block according to the spaces between the pieces. Begin with the narrowest spaces. If no spaces are shown, the pieces can be assembled in any order.

cp 1   cp 1
Cut 4.   Cut 1.

cp 2   cp 2
Cut 16.   Cut 16.

cp 3   cp 4
Cut 4.   Cut 4.

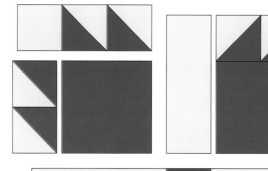

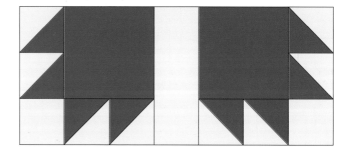

Line
Diagram

Foundation
Pattern

CONFEDERATE ROSE (cr)

Block Assembly

Assemble the block according to the spaces between the pieces. Begin with the narrowest spaces. If no spaces are shown, the pieces can be assembled in any order.

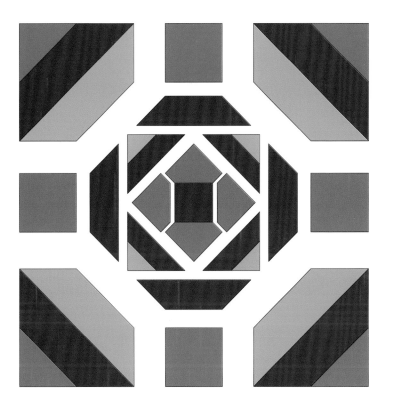

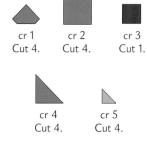

cr 1
Cut 4.

cr 2
Cut 4.

cr 3
Cut 1.

cr 4
Cut 4.

cr 5
Cut 4.

cr 6
Cut 4.

cr 7
Cut 4.

cr 8
Cut 4.

cr 8
Cut 4.

Line
Diagram

Foundation
Pattern

207

CAKE STAND (cs)

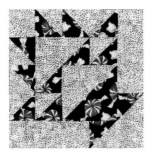

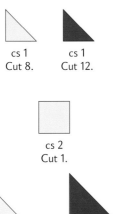

cs 1
Cut 8.

cs 1
Cut 12.

cs 2
Cut 1.

cs 3
Cut 3.

cs 3
Cut 1.

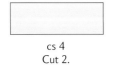

cs 4
Cut 2.

Block Assembly

Assemble the block according to the spaces between the pieces. Begin with the narrowest spaces. If no spaces are shown, the pieces can be assembled in any order.

Line
Diagram

Foundation
Pattern

CHRISTMAS TREE (ct)

Block Assembly

Assemble the block according to the spaces between the pieces. Begin with the narrowest spaces. If no spaces are shown, the pieces can be assembled in any order.

ct 1
Cut 3.

ct 2
Cut 12.

ct 2
Cut 18.

ct 3
Cut 2.

ct 4
Cut 1.

ct 5
Cut 2.

Line Diagram

Foundation Pattern

Rotary Cutting

209

CLOVER LEAF (cv)

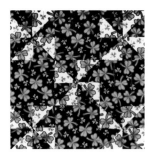

Block Assembly
Assemble the block according to the spaces between the pieces. Begin with the narrowest spaces. If no spaces are shown, the pieces can be assembled in any order.

cv 1
Cut 20.

cv 1
Cut 20.

cv 2
Cut 4.

Line
Diagram

Foundation
Pattern

Block Assembly

Assemble the block according to the spaces between the pieces. Begin with the narrowest spaces. If no spaces are shown, the pieces can be assembled in any order.

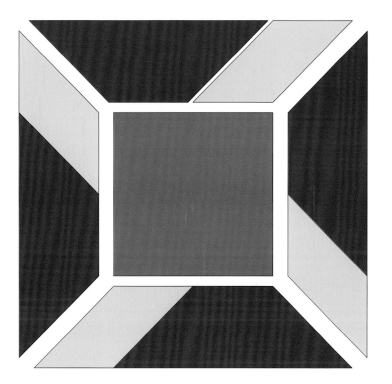

cw 1
Cut 4.

cw 2
Cut 4.

cw 3
Cut 1.

Line
Diagram

Foundation
Pattern

Rotary
Cutting

CRYSTAL STAR (cy)

cy 1
Cut 4.

cy 2
Cut 8.

cy 2
Cut 4.

cy 3
Cut 1.

cy 4
Cut 4.

Block Assembly

Assemble the block according to the spaces between the pieces. Begin with the narrowest spaces. If no spaces are shown, the pieces can be assembled in any order.

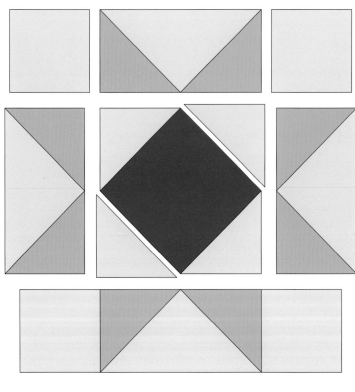

Line
Diagram

Foundation
Pattern

Rotary
Cutting

212

Block Assembly

Assemble the block according to the spaces between the pieces. Begin with the narrowest spaces. If no spaces are shown, the pieces can be assembled in any order.

da 1
Cut 8.

da 2
Cut 4.

da 3
Cut 4.

da 4
Cut 4.

Line
Diagram

Foundation
Pattern

213

Block Assembly

Assemble the block according to the spaces between the pieces. Begin with the narrowest spaces. If no spaces are shown, the pieces can be assembled in any order.

dd 1
Cut 4.

dd 2
Cut 1.

dd 3
Cut 4.

dd 4
Cut 4.

dd 5
Cut 8.

dd 6
Cut 4.

dd 7
Cut 4.

dd 7
Cut 4.

dd 7R
Cut 4.

dd 7R
Cut 4.

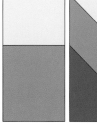
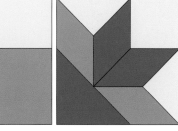

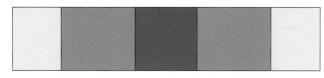

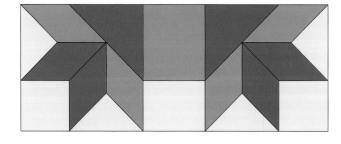

Line
Diagram

Foundation
Pattern

ELSIE'S FAVORITE (ef)

Block Assembly

Assemble the block according to the spaces between the pieces. Begin with the narrowest spaces. If no spaces are shown, the pieces can be assembled in any order.

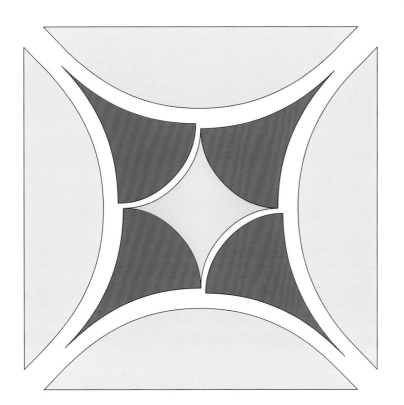

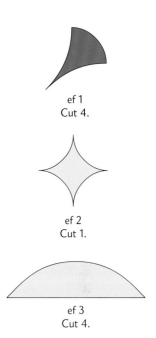

ef 1
Cut 4.

ef 2
Cut 1.

ef 3
Cut 4.

Line
Diagram

215

Block Assembly

Assemble the block according to the spaces between the pieces. Begin with the narrowest spaces. If no spaces are shown, the pieces can be assembled in any order.

eq 1
Cut 4.

eq 2
Cut 4.

eq 2
Cut 1.

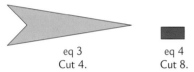

eq 3
Cut 4.

eq 4
Cut 8.

eq 5
Cut 4.

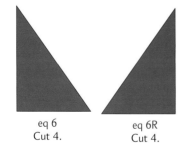

eq 6
Cut 4.

eq 6R
Cut 4.

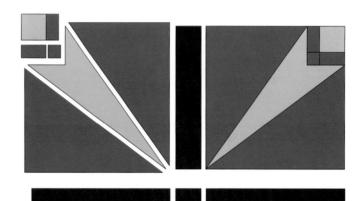

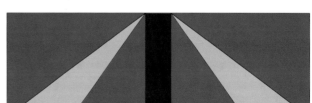

Line
Diagram

Foundation
Pattern

Block Assembly

Assemble the block according to the spaces between the pieces. Begin with the narrowest spaces. If no spaces are shown, the pieces can be assembled in any order.

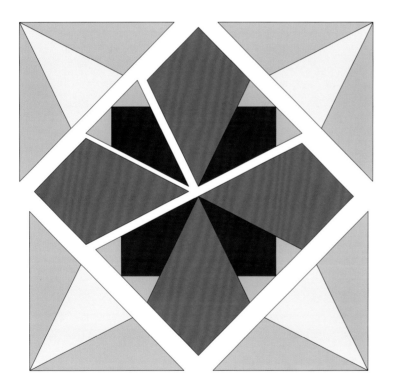

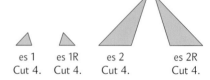

es 1
Cut 4.

es 1R
Cut 4.

es 2
Cut 4.

es 2R
Cut 4.

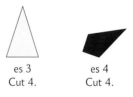

es 3
Cut 4.

es 4
Cut 4.

es 5
Cut 4.

Line
Diagram

Foundation
Pattern

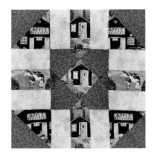

Block Assembly

Assemble the block according to the spaces between the pieces. Begin with the narrowest spaces. If no spaces are shown, the pieces can be assembled in any order.

ev 1
Cut 4.

ev 2
Cut 1.

ev 3
Cut 8.

ev 3
Cut 4.

ev 4
Cut 4.

ev 5
Cut 4.

ev 5
Cut 4.

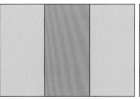

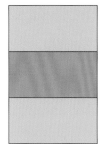

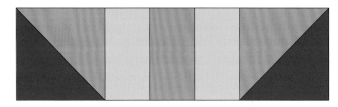

Line
Diagram

Foundation
Pattern

Rotary
Cutting

218

Block Assembly

Assemble the block according to the spaces between the pieces. Begin with the narrowest spaces. If no spaces are shown, the pieces can be assembled in any order.

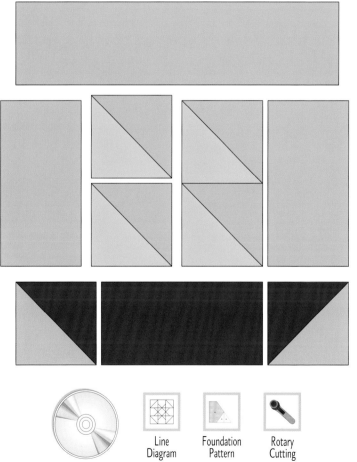

fb 1
Cut 4.

fb 1
Cut 2.

fb 1
Cut 6.

fb 2
Cut 1.

fb 2
Cut 2.

fb 3
Cut 1.

Line
Diagram

Foundation
Pattern

Rotary
Cutting

Block Assembly

Assemble the block according to the spaces between the pieces. Begin with the narrowest spaces. If no spaces are shown, the pieces can be assembled in any order.

fc 1
Cut 20.

fc 1
Cut 20.

fc 2
Cut 4.

fc 3
Cut 8.

fc 3
Cut 8.

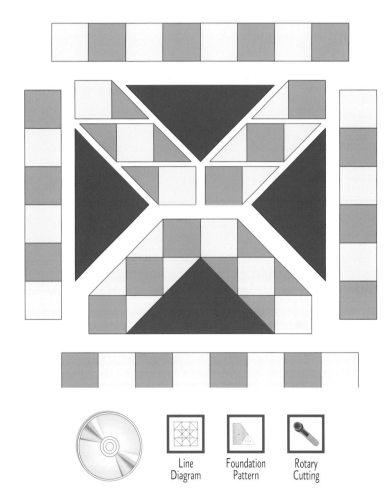

Line
Diagram

Foundation
Pattern

Rotary
Cutting

Block Assembly

Assemble the block according to the spaces between the pieces. Begin with the narrowest spaces. If no spaces are shown, the pieces can be assembled in any order.

fs 1
Cut 4.

fs 2
Cut 1.

fs 3
Cut 8.

fs 3
Cut 4.

fs 4
Cut 4.

Line
Diagram

Foundation
Pattern

Rotary
Cutting

GOOD CHEER (gc)

Block Assembly

Assemble the block according to the spaces between the pieces. Begin with the narrowest spaces. If no spaces are shown, the pieces can be assembled in any order.

gc 1
Cut 4.

gc 1
Cut 8.

gc 1
Cut 12.

gc 2
Cut 8.

gc 2
Cut 8.

gc 3
Cut 8.

gc 4
Cut 4.

gc 4R
Cut 4.

Line
Diagram

Foundation
Pattern

Rotary
Cutting

GIRL'S FAVORITE (gf)

Block Assembly

Assemble the block according to the spaces between the pieces. Begin with the narrowest spaces. If no spaces are shown, the pieces can be assembled in any order.

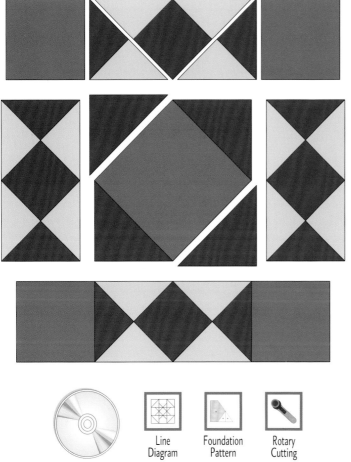

gf 1
Cut 16.

gf 1
Cut 8.

gf 2
Cut 4.

gf 3
Cut 4.

gf 4
Cut 1.

gf 5
Cut 4.

Line Diagram

Foundation Pattern

Rotary Cutting

GIRL'S JOY (gj)

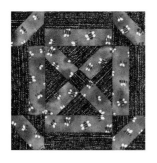

Block Assembly

Assemble the block according to the spaces between the pieces. Begin with the narrowest spaces. If no spaces are shown, the pieces can be assembled in any order.

gj 1
Cut 4.

gj 2
Cut 8.

gj 3
Cut 1.

gj 4
Cut 4.

gj 5
Cut 4.

gj 5
Cut 4.

gj 6
Cut 4.

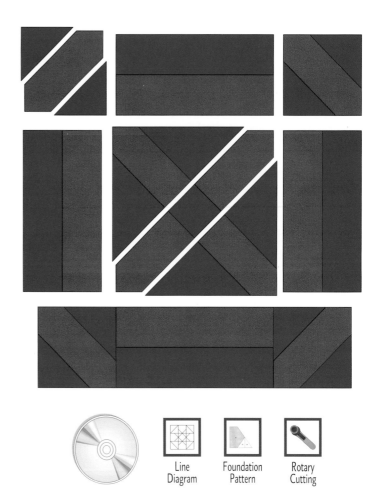

Line
Diagram

Foundation
Pattern

Rotary
Cutting

Block Assembly

Assemble the block according to the spaces between the pieces. Begin with the narrowest spaces. If no spaces are shown, the pieces can be assembled in any order.

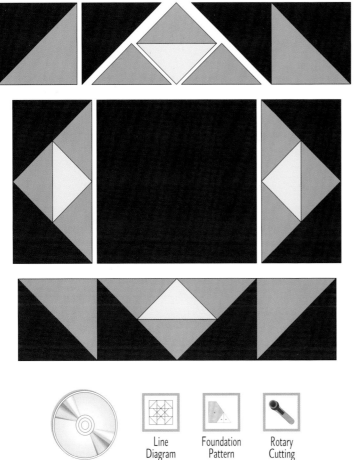

gm 1
Cut 4.

gm 1
Cut 12.

gm 2
Cut 4.

gm 2
Cut 12.

gm 3
Cut 1.

Line Diagram

Foundation Pattern

Rotary Cutting

225

GOLD NUGGETS (gn)

gn 1
Cut 1.

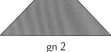

gn 2
Cut 1.

gn 2
Cut 2.

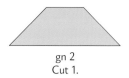

gn 2
Cut 1.

Block Assembly

Assemble the block according to the spaces between the pieces. Begin with the narrowest spaces. If no spaces are shown, the pieces can be assembled in any order.

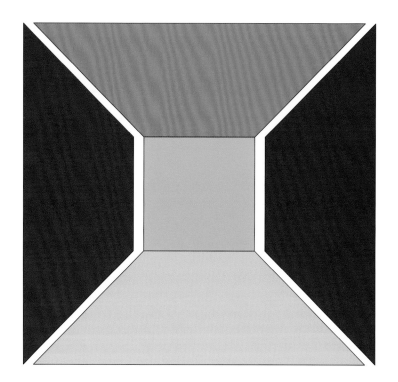

Line
Diagram

Block Assembly

Assemble the block according to the spaces between the pieces. Begin with the narrowest spaces. If no spaces are shown, the pieces can be assembled in any order.

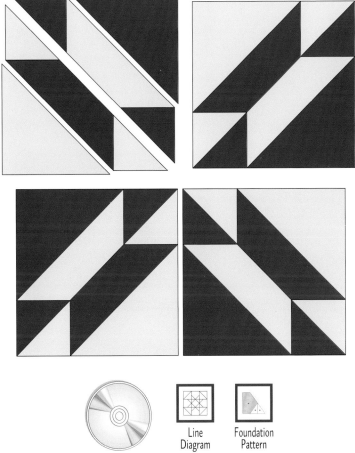

gr 1
Cut 8.

gr 1
Cut 8.

gr 2
Cut 4.

gr 2
Cut 4.

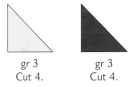

gr 3
Cut 4.

gr 3
Cut 4.

Line
Diagram

Foundation
Pattern

Block Assembly

Assemble the block according to the spaces between the pieces. Begin with the narrowest spaces. If no spaces are shown, the pieces can be assembled in any order.

ha 1
Cut 9.

ha 2
Cut 8.   ha 2
            Cut 8.

ha 3
Cut 12.   ha 3
            Cut 12.

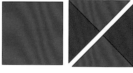 

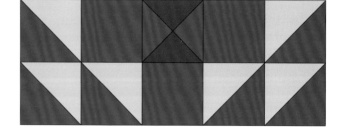

Line
Diagram

Foundation
Pattern

Block Assembly

Assemble the block according to the spaces between the pieces. Begin with the narrowest spaces. If no spaces are shown, the pieces can be assembled in any order.

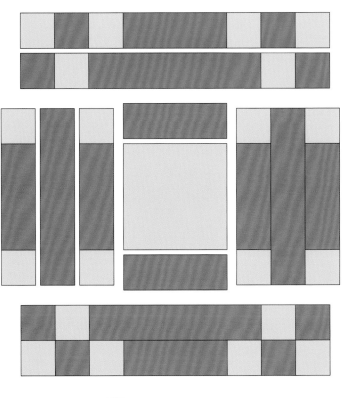

hc 1
Cut 20.

hc 1
Cut 8.

hc 2
Cut 8.

hc 3
Cut 4.

hc 4
Cut 1.

Line
Diagram

Foundation
Pattern

Block Assembly

Assemble the block according to the spaces between the pieces. Begin with the narrowest spaces. If no spaces are shown, the pieces can be assembled in any order.

ht 1
Cut 8.

ht 2
Cut 8.

ht 3
Cut 4.

ht 3
Cut 4.

ht 4
Cut 1.

ht 5
Cut 4.

ht 6
Cut 2.

ht 6R
Cut 2.

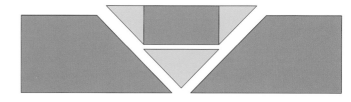

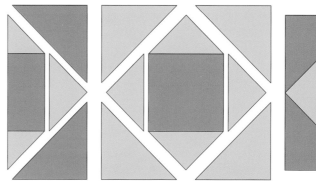

Line
Diagram

Foundation
Pattern

Rotary
Cutting

ICE CREAM BOWL (ic)

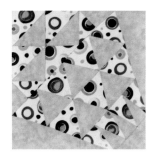

Block Assembly

Assemble the block according to the spaces between the pieces. Begin with the narrowest spaces. If no spaces are shown, the pieces can be assembled in any order.

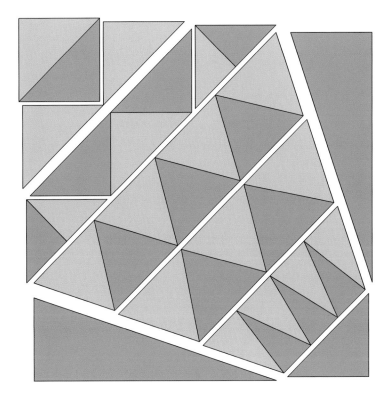

See pages 232 and 233 for the cutting instructions and a numbered assembly diagram for this block.

This block is not for the faint of heart. But the results are delicious. There are twenty-two templates, and only three of them are used more than once. The triangles in the middle three rows look so similar on the CD that we added some extra help with the assembly on the next two pages. Hint: The foundation pattern is a piece of cake (and ice cream).

Line Diagram

Foundation Pattern

231

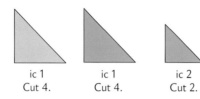

ic 1
Cut 4.

ic 1
Cut 4.

ic 2
Cut 2.

ic 2
Cut 2.

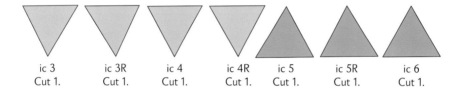

ic 3
Cut 1.

ic 3R
Cut 1.

ic 4
Cut 1.

ic 4R
Cut 1.

ic 5
Cut 1.

ic 5R
Cut 1.

ic 6
Cut 1.

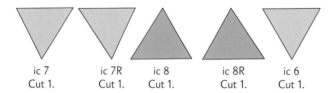

ic 7
Cut 1.

ic 7R
Cut 1.

ic 8
Cut 1.

ic 8R
Cut 1.

ic 6
Cut 1.

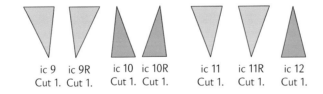

ic 9
Cut 1.

ic 9R
Cut 1.

ic 10
Cut 1.

ic 10R
Cut 1.

ic 11
Cut 1.

ic 11R
Cut 1.

ic 12
Cut 1.

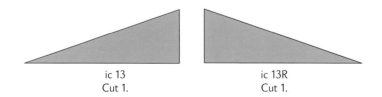

ic 13
Cut 1.

ic 13R
Cut 1.

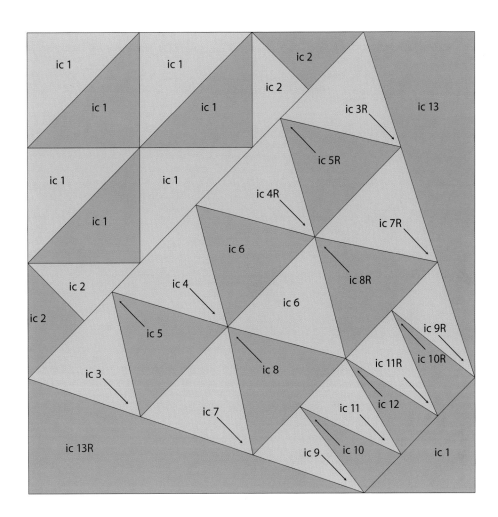

Pin each template to the fabric as you cut the pieces. When you lay out the pieces, point them in the direction indicated by the arrows.

in 1
Cut 1.

in 1
Cut 1.

in 1
Cut 1.

in 2
Cut 1.

in 2
Cut 1.

in 2
Cut 1.

in 2
Cut 6.

in 2
Cut 9.

in 3
Cut 4.

in 3
Cut 1.

in 4
Cut 1.

in 4
Cut 1.

in 5
Cut 1.

in 5
Cut 1.

in 5
Cut 2.

in 5R
Cut 2.

in 6
Cut 2.

in 7
Cut 6.

Block Assembly

Assemble the block according to the spaces between the pieces. Begin with the narrowest spaces. If no spaces are shown, the pieces can be assembled in any order.

See page 278 for a numbered assembly diagram.

Line
Diagram

Foundation
Pattern

Rotary
Cutting

Block Assembly

Assemble the block according to the spaces between the pieces. Begin with the narrowest spaces. If no spaces are shown, the pieces can be assembled in any order.

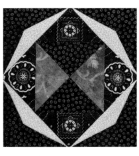

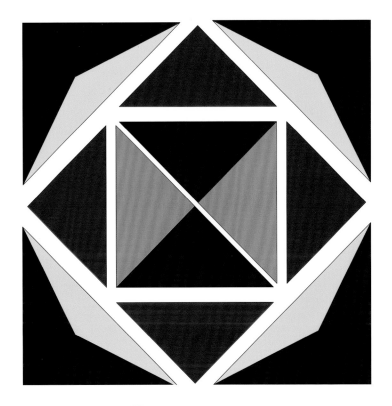

je 1
Cut 4.

je 2
Cut 4.

je 3
Cut 2.

je 3
Cut 2.

je 3
Cut 4.

Line
Diagram

Foundation
Pattern

235

Block Assembly

Assemble the block according to the spaces between the pieces. Begin with the narrowest spaces. If no spaces are shown, the pieces can be assembled in any order.

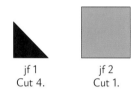

jf 1
Cut 4.

jf 2
Cut 1.

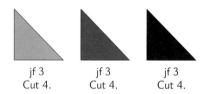

jf 3
Cut 4.

jf 3
Cut 4.

jf 3
Cut 4.

Line
Diagram

Foundation
Pattern

Rotary
Cutting

John's Favorite (jo)

Block Assembly

Assemble the block according to the spaces between the pieces. Begin with the narrowest spaces. If no spaces are shown, the pieces can be assembled in any order.

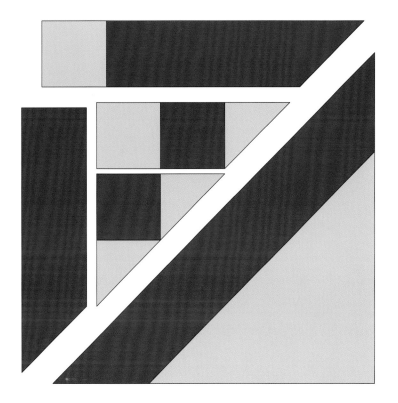

jo 1
Cut 2.

jo 1
Cut 2.

jo 2
Cut 1.

jo 2R
Cut 1.

jo 3
Cut 3.

jo 4
Cut 1.

jo 5
Cut 1.

Line Diagram

Foundation Pattern

237

ks 1
Cut 2.

ks 1
Cut 2.

ks 2
Cut 8.

ks 3
Cut 8.

ks 3R
Cut 8.

ks 4
Cut 4.

ks 5
Cut 4.

Block Assembly

Assemble the block according to the spaces between the pieces. Begin with the narrowest spaces. If no spaces are shown, the pieces can be assembled in any order.

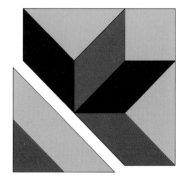

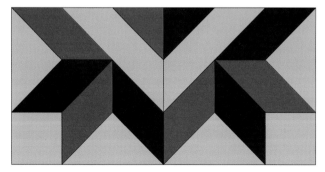

Line
Diagram

Foundation
Pattern

Block Assembly
Assemble the block according to the spaces between the pieces. Begin with the narrowest spaces. If no spaces are shown, the pieces can be assembled in any order.

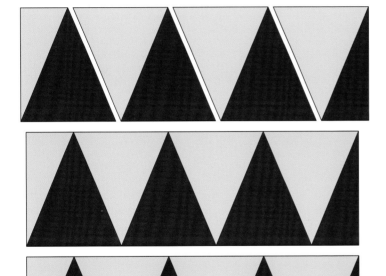

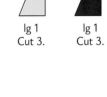

lg 1
Cut 3.

lg 1
Cut 3.

lg 2
Cut 9.

lg 2
Cut 9.

Line
Diagram

Foundation
Pattern

LUCKY STAR (ls)

Block Assembly

Assemble the block according to the spaces between the pieces. Begin with the narrowest spaces. If no spaces are shown, the pieces can be assembled in any order.

See page 279 for a numbered assembly diagram.

ls 1
Cut 4.

ls 1
Cut 4.

ls 2
Cut 4.

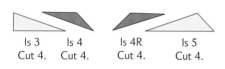

ls 3
Cut 4.

ls 4
Cut 4.

ls 4R
Cut 4.

ls 5
Cut 4.

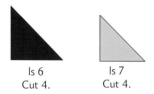

ls 6
Cut 4.

ls 7
Cut 4.

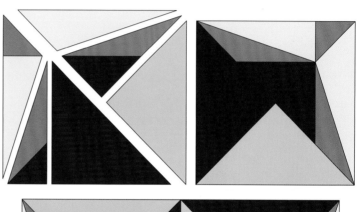

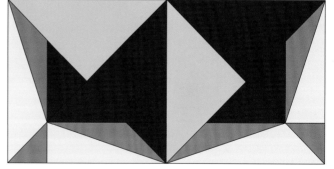

Line
Diagram

Foundation
Pattern

Rotary
Cutting

Block Assembly

Assemble the block according to the spaces between the pieces. Begin with the narrowest spaces. If no spaces are shown, the pieces can be assembled in any order.

See page 278 for a numbered assembly diagram.

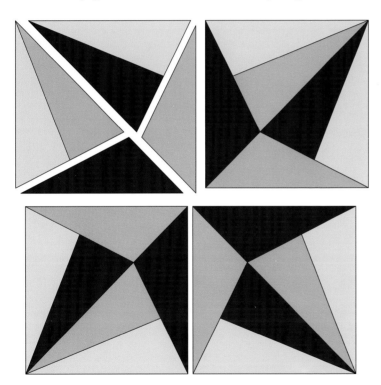

md 1
Cut 4.

md 1R
Cut 4.

md 2
Cut 4.

md 2R
Cut 4.

md 3
Cut 4.

md 3R
Cut 4.

Line
Diagram

Foundation
Pattern

241

MILLER'S DAUGHTER (ml)

ml 1
Cut 8.

ml 2
Cut 2.

ml 3
Cut 8.

ml 4
Cut 8.

ml 5
Cut 2.

Block Assembly

Assemble the block according to the spaces between the pieces. Begin with the narrowest spaces. If no spaces are shown, the pieces can be assembled in any order.

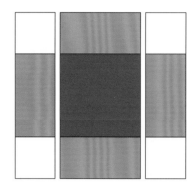

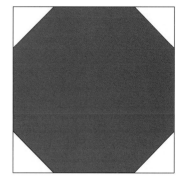

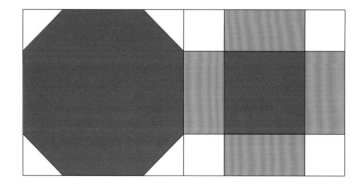

Line
Diagram

Foundation
Pattern

Rotary
Cutting

242

Block Assembly

Assemble the block according to the spaces between the pieces. Begin with the narrowest spaces. If no spaces are shown, the pieces can be assembled in any order.

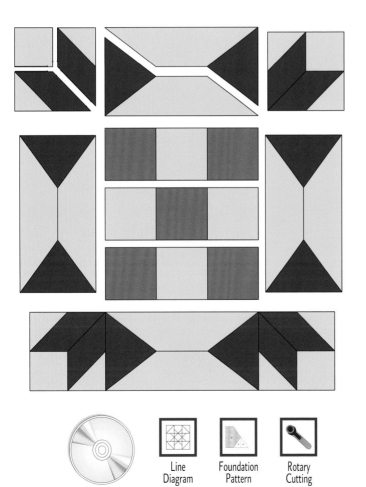

mm 1
Cut 4.

mm 2
Cut 8.

mm 3
Cut 4.

mm 3
Cut 5.

mm 4
Cut 4.

mm 4R
Cut 4.

mm 5
Cut 8.

mm 6
Cut 8.

Line Diagram

Foundation Pattern

Rotary Cutting

243

Minnesota (mn)

mn 1
Cut 8.

mn 1R
Cut 8.

mn 2
Cut 1.

mn 3
Cut 4.

mn 4
Cut 8.

mn 4
Cut 8.

mn 5
Cut 4.

Block Assembly

Assemble the block according to the spaces between the pieces. Begin with the narrowest spaces. If no spaces are shown, the pieces can be assembled in any order.

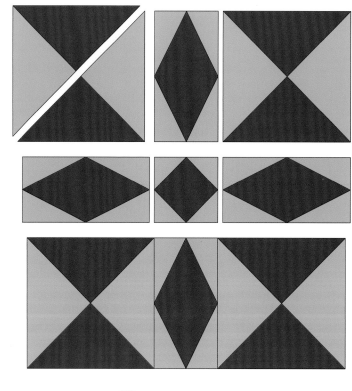

Line
Diagram

Foundation
Pattern

Block Assembly

Assemble the block according to the spaces between the pieces. Begin with the narrowest spaces. If no spaces are shown, the pieces can be assembled in any order.

mq 1
Cut 1.

mq 2
Cut 4.

mq 3
Cut 4.

Line Diagram

Foundation Pattern

Rotary Cutting

MORNING STAR (ms)

ms 1
Cut 24.

ms 1R
Cut 24.

ms 2
Cut 9.

ms 3
Cut 12.

ms 4
Cut 4.

Block Assembly

Assemble the block according to the spaces between the pieces. Begin with the narrowest spaces. If no spaces are shown, the pieces can be assembled in any order.

Line
Diagram

Foundation
Pattern

MAYFLOWER (my)

Block Assembly

Assemble the block according to the spaces between the pieces. Begin with the narrowest spaces. If no spaces are shown, the pieces can be assembled in any order.

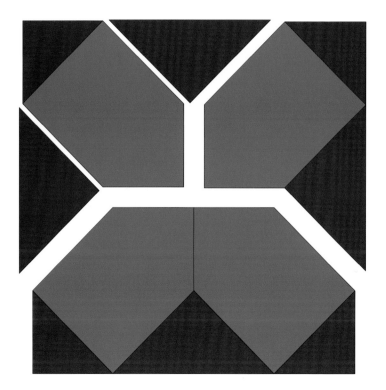

my 1
Cut 4.

my 2
Cut 4.

my 3
Cut 4.

Line
Diagram

Foundation
Pattern

Rotary
Cutting

Block Assembly

Assemble the block according to the spaces between the pieces. Begin with the narrowest spaces. If no spaces are shown, the pieces can be assembled in any order.

nc 1
Cut 28.

nc 2
Cut 10.

nc 2
Cut 8.

nc 3
Cut 4.

Line
Diagram

Foundation
Pattern

Rotary
Cutting

NEXT DOOR NEIGHBOR (nd)

Block Assembly

Assemble the block according to the spaces between the pieces. Begin with the narrowest spaces. If no spaces are shown, the pieces can be assembled in any order.

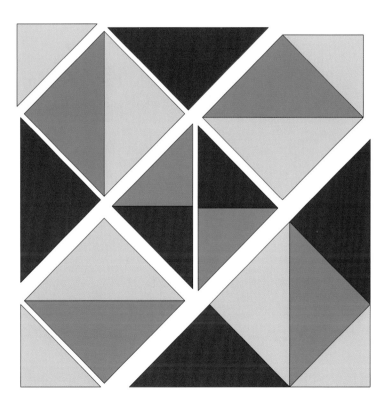

nd 1
Cut 4.

nd 1
Cut 2.

nd 1
Cut 2.

nd 2
Cut 4.

nd 2
Cut 4.

nd 2
Cut 4.

Line
Diagram

Foundation
Pattern

Rotary
Cutting

249

nj 1
Cut 8.

nj 2
Cut 8.

nj 3
Cut 4.

nj 4
Cut 4.

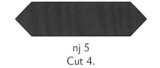

nj 5
Cut 4.

nj 6
Cut 4.

nj 7
Cut 4.

Block Assembly

Assemble the block according to the spaces between the pieces. Begin with the narrowest spaces. If no spaces are shown, the pieces can be assembled in any order.

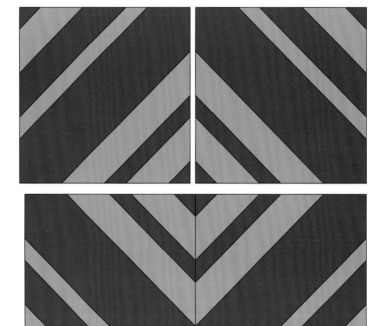

Line
Diagram

Foundation
Pattern

Rotary
Cutting

Block Assembly

Assemble the block according to the spaces between the pieces. Begin with the narrowest spaces. If no spaces are shown, the pieces can be assembled in any order.

np 1
Cut 1.

np 2
Cut 2.

np 3
Cut 14.

np 3
Cut 14.

np 4
Cut 2.

np 5
Cut 1.

Line
Diagram

Foundation
Pattern

251

NORTH STAR (ns)

Block Assembly

Assemble the block according to the spaces between the pieces. Begin with the narrowest spaces. If no spaces are shown, the pieces can be assembled in any order.

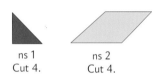

ns 1
Cut 4.

ns 2
Cut 4.

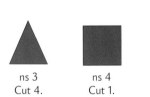

ns 3
Cut 4.

ns 4
Cut 1.

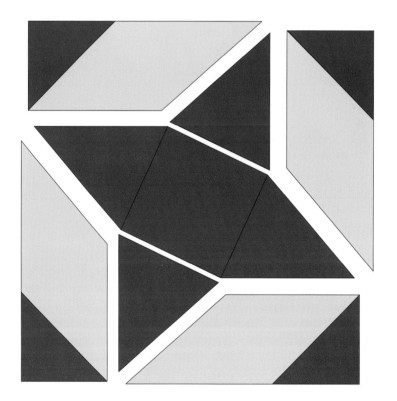

Line
Diagram

Foundation
Pattern

Block Assembly

Assemble the block according to the spaces between the pieces. Begin with the narrowest spaces. If no spaces are shown, the pieces can be assembled in any order.

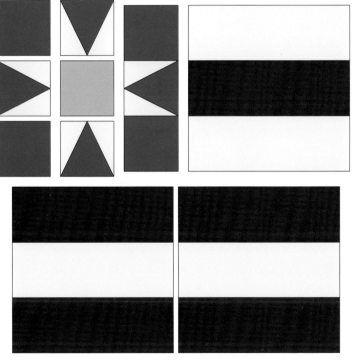

ny 1
Cut 1.

ny 1
Cut 4.

ny 2
Cut 4.

ny 2R
Cut 4.

ny 3
Cut 4.

ny 4
Cut 5.

ny 4
Cut 4.

Line
Diagram

Foundation
Pattern

OLD INDIAN TRAIL (ot)

Block Assembly

Assemble the block according to the spaces between the pieces. Begin with the narrowest spaces. If no spaces are shown, the pieces can be assembled in any order.

ot 1
Cut 12.

ot 1
Cut 12.

ot 2
Cut 2.

ot 2
Cut 2.

ot 3
Cut 2.

ot 4
Cut 1.

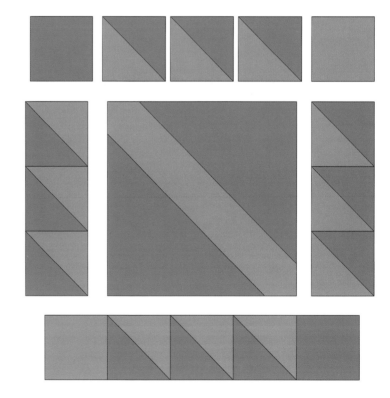

Line
Diagram

Foundation
Pattern

254

PANSY (pa)

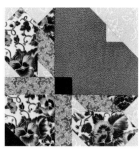

Block Assembly

Assemble the block according to the spaces between the pieces. Begin with the narrowest spaces. If no spaces are shown, the pieces can be assembled in any order.

See page 279 for a numbered assembly diagram.

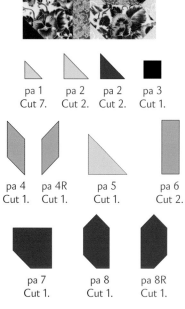

pa 1
Cut 7.

pa 2
Cut 2.

pa 2
Cut 2.

pa 3
Cut 1.

pa 4
Cut 1.

pa 4R
Cut 1.

pa 5
Cut 1.

pa 6
Cut 2.

pa 7
Cut 1.

pa 8
Cut 1.

pa 8R
Cut 1.

pa 9
Cut 1.

pa 9R
Cut 1.

pa 10
Cut 1.

 Line Diagram

 Foundation Pattern

 Rotary Cutting

pc 1
Cut 1.

pc 2
Cut 1.

pc 2
Cut 1.

pc 3
Cut 2.

pc 4
Cut 2.

pc 4R
Cut 2.

pc 5
Cut 3.

pc 5R
Cut 3.

pc 6
Cut 3.

Block Assembly

Assemble the block according to the spaces between the pieces. Begin with the narrowest spaces. If no spaces are shown, the pieces can be assembled in any order.

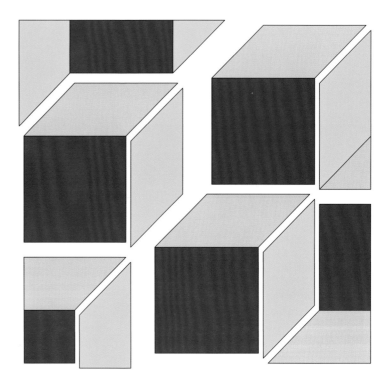

Line
Diagram

Foundation
Pattern

PLEASANT PATHS (pp)

Block Assembly

Assemble the block according to the spaces between the pieces. Begin with the narrowest spaces. If no spaces are shown, the pieces can be assembled in any order.

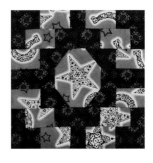

pp 1
Cut 12.

pp 1
Cut 4.

pp 2
Cut 6.

pp 3
Cut 2.

pp 3R
Cut 2.

pp 4
Cut 4.

pp 5
Cut 1.

Line
Diagram

Foundation
Pattern

Block Assembly

Assemble the block according to the spaces between the pieces. Begin with the narrowest spaces. If no spaces are shown, the pieces can be assembled in any order.

See page 279 for a numbered assembly diagram.

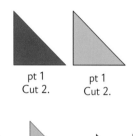

pt 1
Cut 2.

pt 1
Cut 2.

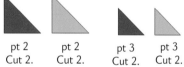

pt 2
Cut 2.

pt 2
Cut 2.

pt 3
Cut 2.

pt 3
Cut 2.

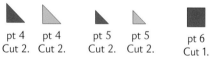

pt 4
Cut 2.

pt 4
Cut 2.

pt 5
Cut 2.

pt 5
Cut 2.

pt 6
Cut 1.

Line
Diagram

Foundation
Pattern

Rotary
Cutting

258

Block Assembly

Assemble the block according to the spaces between the pieces. Begin with the narrowest spaces. If no spaces are shown, the pieces can be assembled in any order.

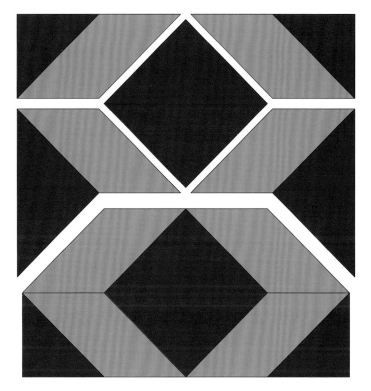

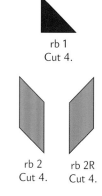

rb 1
Cut 4.

rb 2
Cut 4.

rb 2R
Cut 4.

rb 3
Cut 2.

rb 4
Cut 2.

Line
Diagram

Foundation
Pattern

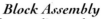

Block Assembly

Assemble the block according to the spaces between the pieces. Begin with the narrowest spaces. If no spaces are shown, the pieces can be assembled in any order.

rc 1
Cut 8.

rc 1
Cut 8.

rc 2
Cut 16.

rc 2
Cut 16.

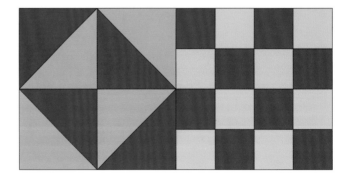

Line
Diagram

Foundation
Pattern

Rotary
Cutting

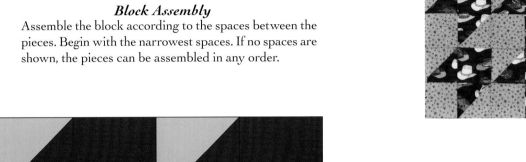

Block Assembly

Assemble the block according to the spaces between the pieces. Begin with the narrowest spaces. If no spaces are shown, the pieces can be assembled in any order.

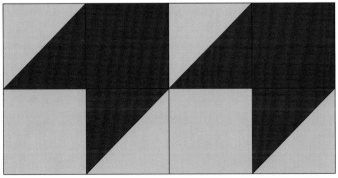

rh 1
Cut 8.

rh 1
Cut 8.

rh 2
Cut 4.

rh 2
Cut 4.

Line Diagram

Foundation Pattern

Rotary Cutting

Block Assembly

Assemble the block according to the spaces between the pieces. Begin with the narrowest spaces. If no spaces are shown, the pieces can be assembled in any order.

rr 1
Cut 4.

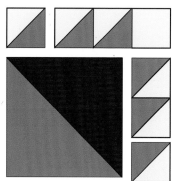

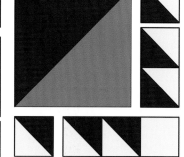

rr 2
Cut 12.

rr 2
Cut 24.

rr 2
Cut 12.

rr 3
Cut 4.

rr 3
Cut 4.

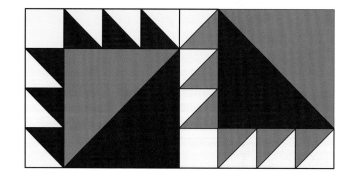

Line
Diagram

Foundation
Pattern

Rotary
Cutting

Block Assembly

Assemble the block according to the spaces between the pieces. Begin with the narrowest spaces. If no spaces are shown, the pieces can be assembled in any order.

rs 1
Cut 4.

rs 2
Cut 1.

rs 3
Cut 4.

rs 4   rs 4R   rs 5   rs 6
Cut 4.   Cut 4.   Cut 4.   Cut 4.

rs 7
Cut 4.

rs 8
Cut 4.

Line
Diagram

Foundation
Pattern

SUGAR BOWL (sb)

Block Assembly

Assemble the block according to the spaces between the pieces. Begin with the narrowest spaces. If no spaces are shown, the pieces can be assembled in any order.

sb 1
Cut 1.

sb 2
Cut 4.

sb 2
Cut 6.

sb 3
Cut 2.

sb 4
Cut 2.

sb 4
Cut 1.

Line
Diagram

Foundation
Pattern

Rotary
Cutting

Block Assembly

Assemble the block according to the spaces between the pieces. Begin with the narrowest spaces. If no spaces are shown, the pieces can be assembled in any order.

sd 1
Cut 4.

sd 1
Cut 5.

sd 2
Cut 24.

sd 2
Cut 8.

sd 3
Cut 4.

sd 4
Cut 4.

Line Diagram

Foundation Pattern

Rotary Cutting

265

SHEEP FOLD (sf)

Block Assembly

Assemble the block according to the spaces between the pieces. Begin with the narrowest spaces. If no spaces are shown, the pieces can be assembled in any order.

sf 1
Cut 8.

sf 2
Cut 8.

sf 3
Cut 2.

sf 4
Cut 2.

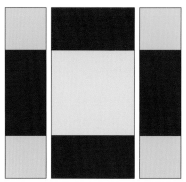

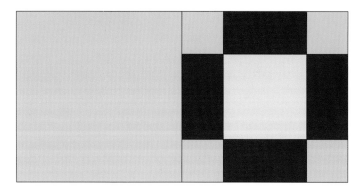

Line
Diagram

Foundation
Pattern

Rotary
Cutting

Block Assembly

Assemble the block according to the spaces between the pieces. Begin with the narrowest spaces. If no spaces are shown, the pieces can be assembled in any order.

sh 1
Cut 9.

sh 1
Cut 9.

sh 2
Cut 1.

sh 3
Cut 1.

Line
Diagram

Foundation
Pattern

Block Assembly

Assemble the block according to the spaces between the pieces. Begin with the narrowest spaces. If no spaces are shown, the pieces can be assembled in any order.

See page 279 for a numbered assembly diagram.

sp 1
Cut 1.

sp 2
Cut 1.

sp 3
Cut 1.

sp 4
Cut 1.

sp 4R
Cut 1.

sp 5
Cut 1.

sp 5R
Cut 1.

sp 6
Cut 1.

sp 6R
Cut 1.

sp 7
Cut 1.

sp 7R
Cut 1.

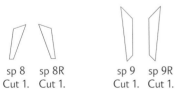

sp 8
Cut 1.

sp 8R
Cut 1.

sp 9
Cut 1.

sp 9R
Cut 1.

Line
Diagram

Foundation
Pattern

Rotary
Cutting

Block Assembly

Assemble the block according to the spaces between the pieces. Begin with the narrowest spaces. If no spaces are shown, the pieces can be assembled in any order.

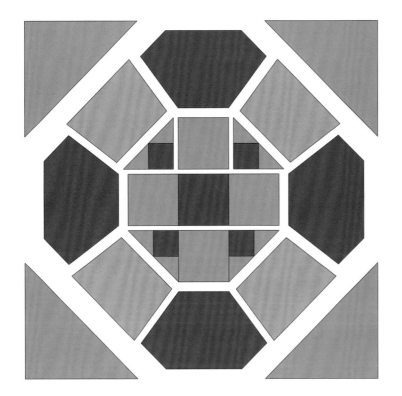

ss 1
Cut 8.

ss 2
Cut 4.

ss 3
Cut 4.

ss 4
Cut 4.

ss 4
Cut 1.

ss 5
Cut 4.

ss 6
Cut 4.

Line
Diagram

Foundation
Pattern

Rotary
Cutting

Block Assembly

Assemble the block according to the spaces between the pieces. Begin with the narrowest spaces. If no spaces are shown, the pieces can be assembled in any order.

su 1
Cut 4.

su 2
Cut 4.

su 3
Cut 4.

su 4
Cut 24.

su 4
Cut 16.

su 5
Cut 1.

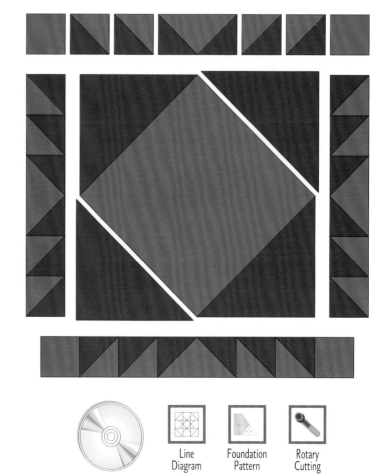

Line Diagram

Foundation Pattern

Rotary Cutting

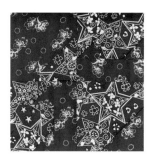

Block Assembly

Assemble the block according to the spaces between the pieces. Begin with the narrowest spaces. If no spaces are shown, the pieces can be assembled in any order.

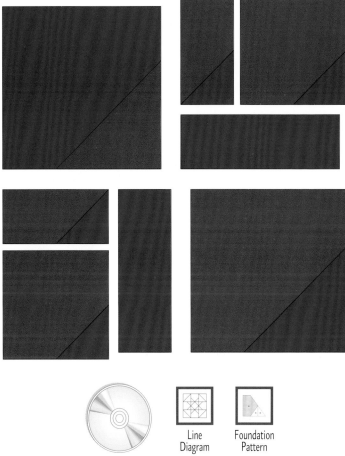

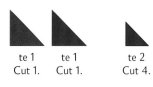

te 1
Cut 1.

te 1
Cut 1.

te 2
Cut 4.

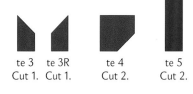

te 3
Cut 1.

te 3R
Cut 1.

te 4
Cut 2.

te 5
Cut 2.

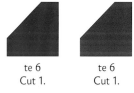

te 6
Cut 1.

te 6
Cut 1.

Line
Diagram

Foundation
Pattern

Block Assembly
Assemble the block according to the spaces between the pieces. Begin with the narrowest spaces. If no spaces are shown, the pieces can be assembled in any order.

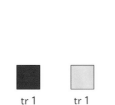

tr 1
Cut 10.

tr 1
Cut 10.

tr 2
Cut 4.

tr 2
Cut 4.

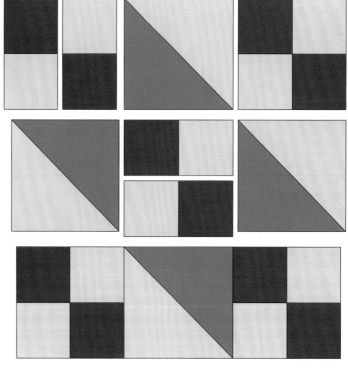

Line
Diagram

Foundation
Pattern

Block Assembly

Assemble the block according to the spaces between the pieces. Begin with the narrowest spaces. If no spaces are shown, the pieces can be assembled in any order.

va 1
Cut 8.

va 2
Cut 4.

va 3
Cut 4.

va 4
Cut 4.

va 5
Cut 1.

va 6
Cut 4.

va 6R
Cut 4.

va 7
Cut 4.

Line Diagram

Foundation Pattern

VERNA BELLE'S FAVORITE (vb)

Block Assembly

Assemble the block according to the spaces between the pieces. Begin with the narrowest spaces. If no spaces are shown, the pieces can be assembled in any order.

See page 279 for a numbered assembly diagram.

vb 1
Cut 4.

vb 2
Cut 4.

vb 2R
Cut 4.

vb 3
Cut 4.

vb 3
Cut 8.

vb 3
Cut 4.

vb 4
Cut 4.

vb 4
Cut 4.

vb 4
Cut 8.

Line
Diagram

Foundation
Pattern

Block Assembly

Assemble the block according to the spaces between the pieces. Begin with the narrowest spaces. If no spaces are shown, the pieces can be assembled in any order.

See page 279 for a numbered assembly diagram.

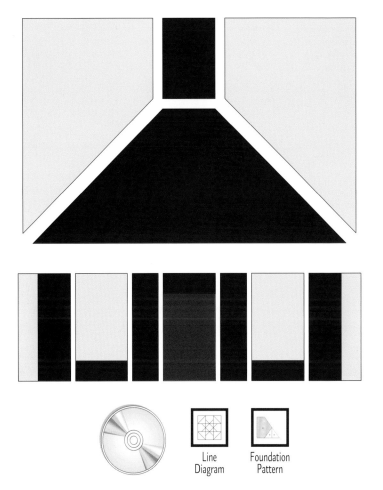

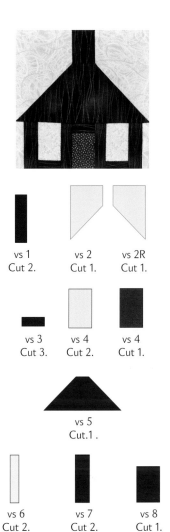

vs 1
Cut 2.

vs 2
Cut 1.

vs 2R
Cut 1.

vs 3
Cut 3.

vs 4
Cut 2.

vs 4
Cut 1.

vs 5
Cut.1 .

vs 6
Cut 2.

vs 7
Cut 2.

vs 8
Cut 1.

Line
Diagram

Foundation
Pattern

Block Assembly

Assemble the block according to the spaces between the pieces. Begin with the narrowest spaces. If no spaces are shown, the pieces can be assembled in any order.

ws 1
Cut 4.

ws 1
Cut 12.

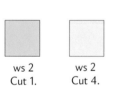

ws 2
Cut 1.

ws 2
Cut 4.

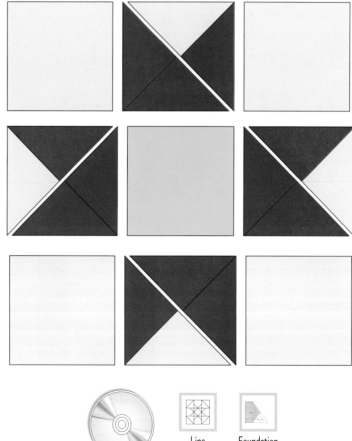

Line
Diagram

Foundation
Pattern

Block Assembly

Assemble the block according to the spaces between the pieces. Begin with the narrowest spaces. If no spaces are shown, the pieces can be assembled in any order.

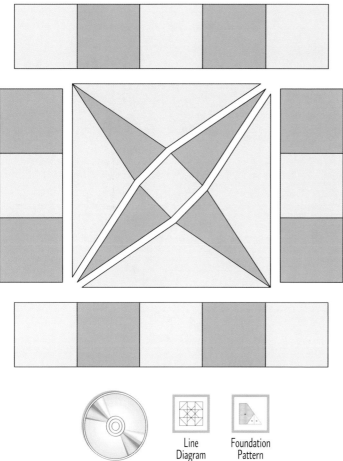

ym 1
Cut 1.

ym 2
Cut 8.

ym 2
Cut 8.

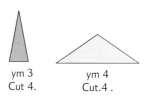

ym 3
Cut 4.

ym 4
Cut.4 .

Line
Diagram

Foundation
Pattern

277

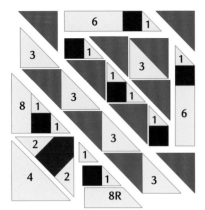

Apple Tree (ap)

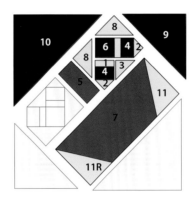

Basket of Flowers (ba)

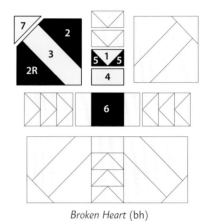

Broken Heart (bh)

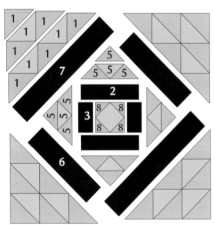

County Fair (cf)

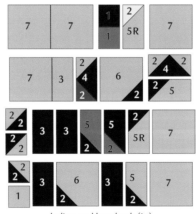

Indian on Horseback (in)

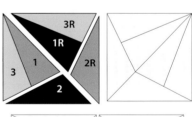

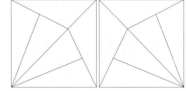

Mother's Delight (md)

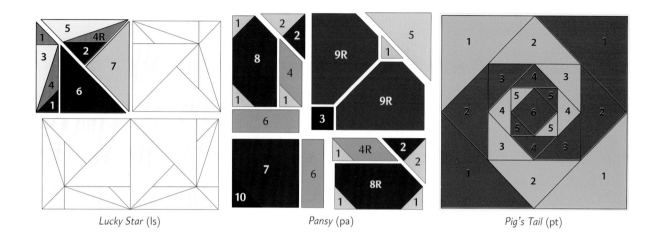

Lucky Star (ls)

Pansy (pa)

Pig's Tail (pt)

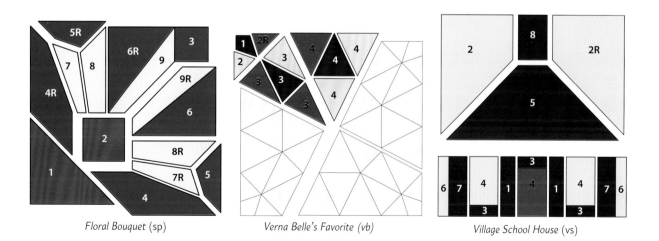

Floral Bouquet (sp)

Verna Belle's Favorite (vb)

Village School House (vs)

ASSEMBLING

YOUR QUILT

Finished Quilt Sizes

Queen 96" × 105"
(king 105" × 105", twin 78" × 96", lap 57" × 66")

Block Sizes

Unfinished size: $8\frac{1}{2}$" × $8\frac{1}{2}$" from raw edge to raw edge
Finished size: 8" × 8"

There will be up to 15% shrinkage in the finished quilt from sewing, quilting, and washing.

Materials

- Scraps for 90 (100, 63, 30) blocks

- Solid gray for cornerstones, inner border, and binding: $1\frac{3}{8}$ yd. ($1\frac{5}{8}$, $1\frac{5}{8}$, $1\frac{1}{8}$)

- Charcoal print for sashing and outer border: $5\frac{1}{8}$ yd. (6, $4\frac{3}{8}$, $2\frac{3}{4}$)

- Backing: $9\frac{3}{4}$ yd. ($9\frac{3}{4}$, 6, 4)

- Batting: 101" × 110" (110" × 110", 82" × 100", 61" × 70")

Cutting Instructions

- From solid gray, cut in the following order:

- 5 (5, 3, 2) strips $1\frac{1}{2}$" wide, across the width of fabric. Cut these strips into 110 (121, 80, 42) $1\frac{1}{2}$" squares for cornerstones.

- 9 (10, 8, 6) strips $1\frac{1}{2}$" wide, across the width of fabric for inner border.

- 11 (12, 10, 7) strips $2\frac{1}{2}$" wide, across the width of fabric for binding.

From charcoal print, cut in the following order:

- 50 (55, 36, 18) strips $1\frac{1}{2}$" wide, across the width of fabric. Cut these strips into 199 (220, 142, 71) $8\frac{1}{2}$" lengths for sashing strips.

- For the queen, king, and twin quilts, cut 4 strips $6\frac{1}{2}$" wide, down the length of the remaining fabric for the outer border. For the lap quilt, cut 4 strips 5" wide, down the length for the outer border.

Quilt Top

Before assembling the quilt top, double check the dimensions of each block to make sure they are $8\frac{1}{2}$" × $8\frac{1}{2}$" from raw edge to raw edge, and adjust as needed. As you make the quilt top, refer to the quilt assembly diagram on page 285.

1. Join 9 (10, 7, 5) blocks alternating with 10 (11, 8, 6) sashing strips to make a block row. Make 10 (10, 9, 6) block rows.

2. Join 9 (10, 7, 5) sashing strips alternating with 10 (11, 8, 6) cornerstones to make a sashing row. Make 11 (11, 10, 7) sashing rows.

3. Sew the sashing rows and block rows together, starting and ending with a sashing row, to complete the blocks and sashing.

Inner Border

1. Sew the 10 (10, 8, 3) $1\frac{1}{2}''$ solid gray inner border strips together, end to end, to make one long strip.

2. Measure the length of the quilt through the center, as shown in figure 1 on page 284. From the long inner-border strip, cut two pieces this measurement.

3. Sew these pieces to the long sides of the quilt, easing the quilt top to fit the border strips.

4. Press all inner- and outer-border seam allowances toward the inner border.

5. Measure the width of the quilt through the center, including the inner border, as shown in figure 2 on page 284.

6. From the long inner-border strip, cut two pieces this measurement.

7. Sew these pieces to the top and bottom of the quilt, easing the quilt top to fit the border strips.

Outer Border

1. Measure the length of the quilt through the center, including the inner border. From the outer-border strips, cut two pieces this measurement. Sew these pieces to the long sides of the quilt.

2. Measure the width of the quilt through the center, including the inner-border strips.

3. From the remaining outer-border strips, cut two pieces this length. Sew these pieces to the top and bottom of the quilt.

Backing

1. Cut the backing yardage into panels of equal length. For the queen size and king size, make three panels, each $3\frac{1}{4}$ yd. long. For the twin size, make two panels, each $2\frac{1}{2}$ yd. long. For the lap size, make two panels, each 2 yd. long.

2. Cut the selvages from the panels, and sew the panels together along their long edges to complete the backing.

Finishing Your Quilt

1. Layer the backing (wrong side up), the batting (either side up), and the quilt top (right side up). Baste the layers together.

2. For quilting, stabilize the quilt sandwich by stitching the layers in the ditch along the sashing rows, starting with a row in the middle of the quilt.

3. Quilt the blocks, using the block designs for inspiration.

4. Stitch in the ditch on both sides of the inner border, and quilt the outer border with a repeating design or radiating straight lines, or quilt as desired.

5. Join the 2½″ solid-gray binding strips together, end to end, to make one long strip. Use your favorite method to bind the edges of the quilt.

6. Sign and label your quilt, and enjoy!

Additional diagrams on the CD.

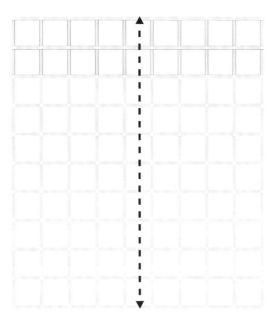

Fig. 1. Measure the length of the quilt through the center.

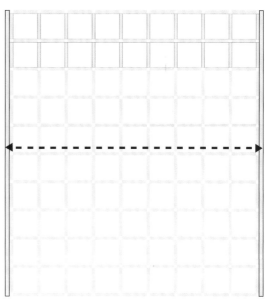

Fig. 2. Measure the width of the quilt through the center, including the inner border.

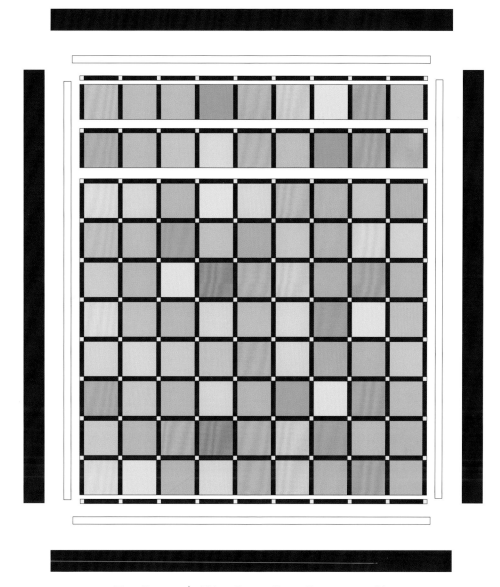

THE FARMER'S WIFE PONY CLUB QUILT assembly

INDEX

Home states of the lucky pony winners

Lucky pony winners and their home states

Meet the Author

This is the second book by best selling quilt author Laurie Aaron Hird. Her first book is *The Farmer's Wife Sampler Quilt*.

A self-taught quilter, Laurie enjoys hand piecing and designing sampler quilts from traditional blocks.

Laurie is an avid and knowledgeable collector of *The Farmer's Wife* magazine, and she owns one of the most complete collections known.

Born and raised in the Los Angeles area of Southern California, she and her family now reside in the beautiful countryside of southwest Wisconsin.

The fonts used here reflect the Art Nouveau influence seen in early issues of *The Farmer's Wife* magazine.

The body text is set in Cochin Roman, selected for its grace and legibility, and the display text is set in Cochin Italic and Cochin Black. This family of fonts echoes the original Cochin, which was designed in 1914 by French type designer Georges Peignot and named after the 18th Century engraver Nicholas Cochin.

Captions and labels are set in Organic, a modern font chosen as a stylish and highly legible complement to the Cochin family.

Printed on archival-quality, acid-free paper.

For ordering information, visit: www.thefarmerswifequilt.com or thefarmerswifequilt.blogspot.com